THE BEST OF The **MAILBOX**® Magazine

Barraclough

Authors

Preschool/Kindergarten

Introduce your students to 33 of today's most acclaimed children's book authors and enrich your curriculum with teacher-tested ideas based on their books. *The Best Of* The Mailbox® *Authors* spotlights authors whose works have proven to be enduring favorites with children and includes literature-based teaching units—selected from issues of *The Mailbox®* magazine preschool and kindergarten editions, published between 1991 and 1997—that provide an abundance of natural connections to content-area learning.

In each author feature you'll find the following:

- Background information to introduce the author
- Brief summaries of several of the author's books
- Cross-curricular classroom activities connected to the featured books
- A list of additional books by the author

Note To The Teacher: *Unless indicated, all of the books featured in this fabulous resource were in print at the time the original magazine articles were published. We've taken care to choose featured units and books for this resource which are currently in print, but cannot guarantee that every book featured will remain in print. Should you have any trouble locating any of the titles featured herein, check with your media specialist.*

Editor:
Kim T. Griswell

Artists:
Pam Crane, Teresa Davidson, Sheila Krill, Rob Mayworth, Donna Teal

Cover Artist:
Kimberly Richard

D1378729

Manufactured in the United States
10 9 8 7 6 5 4 3 2 1

Table Of Contents

Jan Brett

Fairy Tales, Folklore, And Faraway Places

Every book by Jan Brett reflects her unwavering attention to detail and a passion for authenticity. In a world in which far too many things seem mundane, mass-produced, and sacrificed for the bottom line, Jan Brett infuses her books with the painstaking care of a master artisan.

In her childhood Jan Brett often retreated into the pages of beautiful picture books and dreamed of becoming an illustrator. Years later, as a student at the Boston Museum School, she spent hours in the Museum of Fine Arts. Today she finds inspiration in the stories she heard as a child, the art and architecture of foreign countries, and the people and pets in her life.

One of her pets, Little Pearl, was the model for the mouse seen in the artwork on this page and the following four pages from Jan Brett's *Goldilocks And The Three Bears.* The model for Goldilocks (seen on pages 5 and 6) was an adventuresome little girl named Miriam. Folklore and fairy tales have captured the imagination of Jan Brett since she was a little girl herself. In her interpretation of this beloved tale, she showcases several of her trademarks—traditional European costuming, a resilient and resourceful heroine, brilliant border artwork, and animals so real you can practically see their whiskers twitch.

Use the suggestions and reproducibles that follow (on pages 4–9) to introduce your youngsters to *Goldilocks And The Three Bears* and several other Jan Brett books. Sure, these books seem like entirely too much fun to be educational—but that's when the best learning happens!

The First Dog

Published by Harcourt Brace Jovanovich

Perky Pumpkin is the name of Jan Brett's expressive Siberian husky. After marveling at all the different expressions her dog made and viewing Ice Age artifacts and cave drawings, Jan wrote and illustrated *The First Dog.*

Explain to your children that this story is one person's idea of how the first relationship between a human and a dog might have evolved. After reading aloud *The First Dog,* have students scrutinize the pictures of the wolf. Ask youngsters to describe each expression. Find out if they have ever noticed similar expressions on the faces of their pets. For several of the larger pictures of the wolf, have youngsters dictate what the animal might have said if it could have talked. As they dictate, write the comments on paper cut to resemble speech balloons. Use paper clips to attach the speech balloons near the corresponding picture of the wolf. Then flip through the book and read the wolf's comments.

Spray a length of bulletin board paper with faux granite paint. When the paint has dried, cut the paper in the shape of a boulder and attach it to a bulletin board. After studying the illustrations on the borders of this book, have each student draw on the boulder what he would have drawn on a cave wall if he had lived during the Ice Age.

The Twelve Days Of Christmas

Published by G. P. Putnam's Sons

Hoping to inject new vibrancy into a traditional English carol, Jan Brett created her own version of *The Twelve Days Of Christmas.* But she also injected this edition with more substance than first meets the eye. After reading the story aloud to your youngsters or singing it with them, point out that 11 of the two-page spreads contain the words Merry Christmas written in different languages. In Spanish, for example, Merry Christmas is Feliz Navidad. Play a recording of "Feliz Navidad" by José Feliciano (one source is *The Time-Life Treasury Of Christmas*) and translate (or have a Spanish-speaking colleague translate) the Spanish words for your youngsters. Soon everyone will be singing in another language. Feliz Navidad!

Pair your youngsters or divide them into small groups for this big-book activity. In advance, use a photocopier to enlarge 13 copies of Jan Brett's border on page 8. Referring to the verses in *The Twelve Days Of Christmas,* program each page with a numerical phrase from the book. Use a glue stick to mount each page on red or green tagboard. Also locate a sponge cutout that corresponds with each numerical phrase. Have pairs or groups of students use paint and the sponge cutouts to illustrate each phrase. Encourage youngsters to sign their work. When the paint is dry, sing "The Twelve Days Of Christmas" as a group while students display the appropriate page for each verse. Compile these pages into a booklet, and bind them sequentially beneath a cover made from the remaining page.

Before putting Jan Brett's *The Twelve Days Of Christmas* on your classroom library shelf for everyone to enjoy, be sure to mention that she whimsically sees herself as the goose in the white babushka (folded kerchief head covering) in the illustration for "Six geese a-laying."

The Mitten
Published by G. P. Putnam's Sons

Three teachers mentioned to Jan Brett that she should adapt and illustrate the Ukrainian folktale *The Mitten*. And what a splendid idea that turned out to be! Before she began working, a Ukrainian woman translated different versions of the story into English for her. At the Ukrainian Museum in New York City, Jan learned that many children in the Ukraine wear hand-me-downs. So she decided to outfit the child in the story with oversized clothes. She also learned that it's a Ukrainian custom to hang a water jug on a fence so that passersby can get a drink and that a stork's nest on a cottage roof is believed to bring good luck. After reading the story aloud, help students locate the Ukraine on a map. Then explain the significance of the jug and the stork's nest, and have youngsters reexamine the book to look for these elements.

Traditionally, variations of this story have centered around mittens or pots that accommodated the animals. Ask your youngsters to think of other things that could have sheltered several animals. Also invite students to brainstorm catastrophes other than a bear's sneeze that could have sent the animals flying everywhere. Have students dictate and illustrate a new version of this old, old tale.

What ever happened to those teachers who suggested that Jan write this book? Well, whenever a child opens Jan Brett's *The Mitten,* he can read their names on the dedication page. Tad Beagley, the fourth person to whom the book is dedicated, was the model for Nicki. Did you notice the mouse? She was drawn to look like Jan's pet mouse, Little Pearl.

Berlioz The Bear
Published by G. P. Putnam's Sons

The dedication in this Reading Rainbow Book is simply "To Joe." Joseph Hearne airbrushes the backgrounds of Jan Brett's books with a fine spray of paint. But Joe is much more than an artistic accomplice. He's Brett's husband, the model for Berlioz, and probably her number one fan. Joe is a bassist in the Boston Symphony Orchestra. Together the couple travels the world. Not too long ago they visited Bavaria, where Jan found the inspiration for the scenes and costumes in *Berlioz The Bear.*

If you're planning a musical outing, use *Berlioz The Bear* to pique students' interest, or use it as an amusing follow-up to a music-related field trip. At the conclusion of the book, ask students to determine what musical piece Berlioz played as an encore. Play a recording of Rimsky-Korsakov's "Flight Of The Bumblebee," and have youngsters take turns pretending to be a bumblebee as the music plays. Send each youngster home with a copy of one of the Berlioz bookmarks on page 9.

Take another look at the illustrations of the orchestra in *Berlioz The Bear.* A group of musicians posed as models for the scenes in the book. Ask your students if they can imagine the models' reactions to the finished illustrations.

From GOLDILOCKS AND THE THREE BEARS by Jan Brett, copyright ©1987 by Jan Brett. Reprinted by permission of Penguin Putnam Books for Young Readers.

Annie And The Wild Animals

Published by Houghton Mifflin

If your youngsters are studying the seasons, *Annie And The Wild Animals* is an excellent read-aloud choice. In this story, Annie's cat becomes unusually antisocial and wanders off into the wilderness, leaving Annie lonely indeed. Observant readers can scan the detailed borders to find out what's happening in the woods around Annie as she tries to lure another animal for a pet.

After reading the book aloud, have youngsters closely examine the pictures in the first half of the book. Ask them to describe the setting. Then have children describe the changes in the setting as they examine the second half of the book. Ask students to name each season represented in the book.

Trouble With Trolls

Published by G. P. Putnam's Sons

Have you noticed that those little troll dolls have begun to reappear after many, many years in hiding? Jan Brett's newest book is about a little girl who is confronted by trolls (no relation to the plastic-and-fur ones) that want her dog for a pet. With creativity and spunk she helps the trolls find the perfect pet—and it's not her dog. As you're reading this book, be on the lookout for one of Jan Brett's favorite animals! When you've read the story aloud, provide fake fur scraps and construction paper and ask students to create trolls of their own. Encourage them to make pets for their trolls too.

Goldilocks And The Three Bears
Published by G. P. Putnam's Sons

In this version of a familiar old folktale, Jan Brett showcases mousy artwork inspired by her pet mouse, Little Pearl, and the timeless beauty of a little girl who in real life is named Miriam. Notice that in this version Goldilocks isn't said to be as lost as she supposedly was in earlier versions. As you can see by reading several of Jan Brett's books, she is fond of resilient heroines, such as Goldilocks.

It's Jan's intention to "leave young readers with a positive feeling about trying new experiences." Read aloud *Goldilocks And The Three Bears.* Then keep the illustrator's intentions in mind as you lead youngsters in a discussion about Goldilocks' curiosity and adventuresome nature. Would your youngsters have entered an unoccupied cottage? Why or why not?

Show youngsters each of the illustrations again. If possible, project the pictures onto a screen with the use of an opaque projector. In each illustration, locate and discuss the mouse or mice shown. As your youngsters examine picture after picture of the mice, talk about the unfolding secondary story involving them. From the border pictures, have youngsters determine the sequence of planting and tending crocuses. Then provide the supplies for youngsters to plant and tend crocuses of their own.

The Wild Christmas Reindeer
Published by G. P. Putnam's Sons

Jan Brett was having some trouble from her horse, Westminster, about the time she had decided to write a book about the North Pole. She noticed that when she was demanding with "Westy," he tended to balk. But when she spoke calmly to him, he was much more likely to comply. With a change of setting and characters, Jan Brett converted her own real-life experiences into the story of a reindeer handler named Teeka. In preparation for doing the artwork, Jan visited Norway, where a stave church inspired her design of the reindeer barn. She also photographed some very affectionate caribou at the University of Maine in preparation for illustrating the book.

The first date that appears in the book's borders is December 1. That's not only an appropriate starting point for a Christmas book, it's also Jan Brett's birthday. Another look at the borders of this book reminds us of the appeal of handcrafted gifts. Call your youngsters' attention to the things that the elves are making. Ask them to vote for their favorite elf project of those shown in the book. Then assist students as they create a simplified version of the most popular project. Photograph students at work and display the pictures in a pretty tower cutout similar to a tower in the book's borders.

Jan Brett welcomes and replies to mail from teachers and children. As a courtesy to the author, it's best to send either one letter from the class or to package individual student letters in a single large envelope.

Jan Brett
132 Pleasant Street
Norwell, MA 02061

From BERLIOZ THE BEAR by Jan Brett, copyright ©1991 by Jan Brett.
Reprinted by permission of Penguin Putnam Books for Young Readers.

Note To Teacher: Use with suggestion in The Twelve Days Of Christmas on page 4.

I'm
in tune
with reading.

Ask me about
Berlioz The Bear
by
Jan Brett.

**Let's get moving!
I'm ready
to hear
another book
by
Jan Brett.**

A Bouquet Of Books
By Eve Bunting

Eve Bunting's bountiful bouquet of literature is made up of over 100 children's books—a mixture of stories about special days, special people, and special interests. This Irish-born author jots down her seeds of inspiration on just about anything, including a play program and a small airline sickness bag! Then her fertile mind goes to work to cultivate her ideas until beautiful stories with special messages blossom. Why not share a book from Bunting's bouquet with your class? Youngsters will blossom with delight!

Flower Garden
Illustrated by Kathryn Hewitt
Published by Harcourt Brace & Company

In this story, a garden-on-the-go finds a special place in the home and hearts of a loving family. After reading the story, invite each child to create a flower-box garden of his own. To make a flower box, have the child use paint pens to decorate the sides of an empty plastic hand-wipes container (with the lid removed). After the paint dries, have him fill his box with potting soil, then transplant a few flowering plants into the box. Encourage the child to take his flower box home to give to a special person.

A Perfect Father's Day
Illustrated by Susan Meddaugh
Published by Clarion Books

Susie fills her dad's special day with treats inspired by her own favorite things. Help each child highlight special times with his dad (or a male friend) with this activity. For each child, duplicate the cake pattern on page 30 on construction paper. After reading the story, prompt youngsters to discuss things they like to do with their dads (or other significant men). Then have each child cut out a cake pattern and the number of construction-paper candles equal to his age. Have him glue the candles onto his cutout. On the back, have the child illustrate an activity he enjoys sharing with his dad, then write/dictate a sentence about his illustration. Invite each child to give his card to his dad on Father's Day. A perfect card for a perfect day!

Sunflower House
Illustrated by Kathryn Hewitt
Published by Harcourt Brace & Company

Imaginations flourish as a young boy and his friends enjoy the shelter of a homegrown sunflower house. Read this story aloud; then spark imaginations with a student-created sunflower house. To prepare, cut the top and bottom flaps off a large appliance box. Along the bottom cut a few inverted *V* openings large enough for youngsters to fit through. Invite each child to paint and initial a green, leafy stem along a side of the box. Then have her make a construction-paper sunflower to attach to the top of her stem. Put the resulting sunflower house in the dramatic-play center. Invite students to play in the house, prompting them to use their imaginations and a variety of props in their play. What blooming good fun!

The Wednesday Surprise

Illustrated by Donald Carrick
Published by Clarion Books

Anna and Grandma read together every Wednesday to prepare a super surprise for Dad's birthday. After sharing the story and its surprising conclusion, breathe some surprise into this letter-recognition activity. Explain to a small group of students that knowing the letters and their sounds is important in reading. Fog the front surface of a large, acrylic picture frame with your breath; then finger-write a letter on the fog. Challenge youngsters to name the letter before the writing disappears. Then ask them to name words beginning with that letter sound. After several rounds, invite each child in turn to write a breath letter for the others to name. Use a spray glass-cleaner and paper towel to clean the frame between youngsters' turns. What a fun way to give fresh breath to basic skills practice!

Market Day

Illustrated by Holly Berry
Published by Joanna Cotler Books

On the first Thursday of each month, the streets of a small Irish village are filled with activity, excitement, and lots of fun—it's Market Day! After reading this story, have youngsters compare the Market Day sights and events to their own shopping experiences. Then invite youngsters to create their own Market Day. Ask each child to make one or two craft items—such as a musical instrument or an animal model—using an assortment of craft materials. Display the craft goods in several areas in the room. Divide the class into small groups of students. Invite one group to shop, giving a penny to each child in that group with which to buy one item. Have the students in another group tend the market areas, collecting the pennies for purchases in small containers. Rotate the groups so that each has the opportunity to tend the booths and to shop. Then ask each group to count the pennies in a container. It's Market Day!

Our Teacher's Having A Baby

Illustrated by Diane de Groat
Published by Clarion Books

Enthusiasm and anxiety build as a class anticipates the arrival of their teacher's baby. But after the baby's birth, the students wonder if the new mother will continue to be their teacher. Read this story aloud; then lead students to discuss how a woman can be both a mother and a teacher. Ask youngsters to tell about the different roles their own mothers perform. Then invite each child to illustrate her mother on a plain, legal-size envelope. Program the envelope flap with "My mother is a mom, but she is also a...." Ask the child to illustrate one or more envelope-sized sheets of paper, each with a picture representing a different role her mother plays. Have the child write/dictate a completion to the sentence for each illustrated page, then slip the pages into her envelope. During group time, invite each child to share the contents of her envelope. Wow! Mothers can be anything!

More Bunting Books About...

Special Occasions

A Turkey For Thanksgiving
Illustrated by Diane de Groat
Published by Clarion Books

(All Illustrated by Jan Brett)
Happy Birthday, Dear Duck
Published by Clarion Books

Scary, Scary Halloween
Published by Scholastic Inc.

The Valentine Bears
Published by Scholastic Inc.

The Mother's Day Mice
Published by Scholastic Inc.

Social Issues

Someday A Tree
Illustrated by Ronald Himler
Published by Clarion Books

Going Home
Illustrated by David Diaz
Published by Joanna Cotler Books

Smoky Night
Illustrated by David Diaz
Published by Harcourt Brace & Company

Fly Away Home
Illustrated by Ronald Himler
Published by Clarion Books

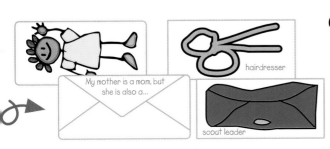

My mother is a mom, but she is also a...

hairdresser

scout leader

On The Move With

Virginia Lee Burton painstakingly created the illustrations for each of her classics. While creating each book, she pinned the first drafts of her illustrations one after another to her studio walls. In this way, she could see the book as a whole, and gradually replace the first drafts with rough and then finished illustrations. She often filled wastebaskets full of what others might well have considered satisfactory work. Only after all the artwork was complete would she generate the text. For her rhythmic watercolor illustrations in *The Little House,* she was awarded the 1943 Caldecott Medal.

Browse through the pages of a Virginia Lee Burton book and you're sure to find plenty of action! The flowing, swirling lines of Burton's illustrations give movement to the staggering tasks of her mechanical heroes. Burton's characters will captivate youngsters with intriguing tales of courage and perseverance. **Climb aboard!**

Katy And The Big Snow
Snowbound!

Becoming snowbound is sure to stir up a flurry of excitement in your classroom! To set a snowy scene, cut large snowdrifts from white bulletin board paper; then, attach the cutouts to the bottom halves of your classroom windows. Before reading *Katy And The Big Snow* orally, have youngsters gaze at the windows and pretend to be snowbound at school. Have youngsters brainstorm a list of reasons why cars, trucks, and buses come and go from school. Then have them discuss how the snow might impede the vehicles' movement and affect the daily schedule. Then, as youngsters sip hot chocolate, read the story aloud. As a follow-up, compare the events that happened in Geoppolis to those the youngsters imagined.

Katy To The Rescue

Nothing could stop Katy! She plowed the city out from under a thick blanket of snow. Youngsters can call on Katy to help with these snowy projects, too. For each child, identically cut two sheets of white construction paper to resemble a snowdrift. Staple each cut-out pair across the top. Have each youngster fold back the top cutout, then, on the second cutout, illustrate what he would have Katy dig out from a big snowdrift. Then have him fold down the top cutout and glue Styrofoam packing pieces to it. Mount youngsters' completed projects side by side. Add a Katy cutout and the title "Katy To The Rescue." Passersby can lift the snowdrifts to see what Katy would uncover. "Hurrah for Katy!"

Mapping Katy's Route

Katy traveled north, south, east, and west—all over Geoppolis—to save the city! Your youngsters will delight in tracing Katy's route with this classroom-sized map. Decorate an empty, eight-ounce milk carton to represent each of the following buildings: Highway Department, Police Department, U.S. Post Office, Railway Station, Telephone Company, Electric Company, Water Department, hospital, Fire Department, and airport. If desired create additional buildings and houses. Using the map of Geoppolis in the book as a guide, arrange the labeled cartons around the classroom to match. As you reread the story, have youngsters form a line, then pretend to be snow plows and follow Katy along her route. Also use this activity to lead learning in other related directions such as an introduction to *north, south, east,* and *west* or community helpers.

Virginia Lee Burton

The Little House
A Booklet For All Seasons

The Little House provides youngsters with the perfect introduction to the seasons. Follow up the reading of the story with a discussion of the seasons. Then have each youngster create his own seasons booklet. Using light blue construction paper, have youngsters follow the directions below to complete each of four pages; then staple their completed pages between construction paper covers.

- **spring**—Draw and color the Little House. Sponge print brown tree trunks and green leaves and grass. Use pink paint to make fingerprint apple blossoms.
- **summer**—Draw and color the Little House. Sponge print brown tree trunks and green leaves and grass. Use white paint to create a field of fingerprint daisies in the grass and red paint to make fingerprint apples on the trees.
- **fall**—Draw and color the Little House. Sponge print brown grass and tree trunks. Use red, yellow, orange, and brown paint to make fingerprint leaves.
- **winter**—Draw and color the Little House. Sponge print brown tree trunks and white snow. Add glue and clear glitter for highlights.

Teresa Tretbar—Gr. K, Roseland Park Elementary, Picayune, MS

My Own Little House

The Little House sat upon a serene, country hill for many years until the city slowly overtook her peaceful setting. As a follow-up to the story, have youngsters predict how the passage of time is likely to affect their own houses. Have each youngster fold a 12" x 18" sheet of art paper in half. On the left side, have him draw and color his house as it looks today. On the right side, have him draw and color his house as he thinks it will look 20 years from now. Label each drawing with the appropriate date; then have each youngster dictate a sentence about what the future holds for his house as you write it below his illustrations. "My, how time flies!"

Denise Hazlerigs, Hodge Elementary
Denton, TX

My Favorite Season

Round out the reading of *The Little House* with this follow-up activity. Duplicate student copies of a house and tree pattern on white construction paper. Have each child cut out the circle. Assist each child in completing the sentence; then have him color the illustration to match. On a bulletin board, have youngsters display their completed cutouts to create a class graph titled "Our Favorite Seasons." Have youngsters refer to the graph to determine their most and least favorite seasons.

Making Progress

The Little House provides youngsters with a pictorial history of transportation. Have youngsters take another look through the pages of the book, noting the different types of transportation represented. Ask youngsters to compare the types of transportation used at the beginning of the story to those at the end of the story. Have youngsters evaluate each mode of transportation for speed, comfort, air pollution, and noise pollution. Then have students predict what types of transportation people may use in the future and any problems that these new modes of transportation might create. "I'm late for school today because my mom's shuttle wouldn't blast off."

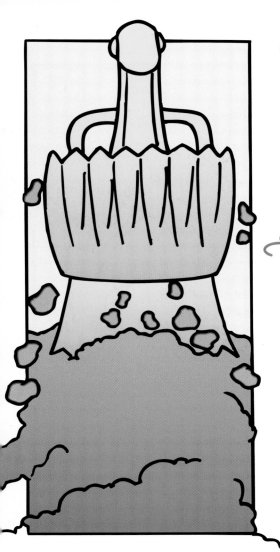

Mike Mulligan And His Steam Shovel

No Way Out

Mike Mulligan and his steam shovel, Mary Anne, dug so fast and so well that they forgot to leave a way out. Stop before reading aloud the end of the story to test youngsters' problem-solving skills. Have youngsters brainstorm a list of solutions to Mike and Mary Anne's problem as you list them on a chart. Have each youngster illustrate his favorite solution. Display the illustrations on a wall before reading the ending of the story aloud. "My, what clever solutions to Popperville's problem!"

Jan Ross—Media Specialist, Dixie Elementary Magnet School, Lexington, KY

Not Just Scrap Metal

The new gasoline, electric, and Diesel motor shovels took jobs away from steam shovels like Mary Anne. Fortunately, Mike Mulligan believed that Mary Anne was still valuable and wouldn't sell her for junk or leave her out to rust. Later the little boy's plan to turn Mary Anne into a furnace for the new town hall also proved that old things have value and can often be used again for new purposes. Challenge your youngsters to reuse throwaway items with this creative thinking project. Give each youngster an empty orange juice can; then have youngsters brainstorm a list of possible uses for the cans as you list them on a chart. As a group, select one use; then have each youngster create a treasure from what might have become trash.

Choo Choo

All By Myself

Choo Choo grows tired of the humdrum task of pulling trains from the country to the city and back again. Determined that she could go much faster and easier by herself, Choo Choo takes off on an adventure in which her best intentions go terribly awry. After reading the story aloud, ask youngsters to share stories of similar experiences. Youngsters may wish to relate tales about times they did things that they knew they weren't supposed to do or stories about times they got lost. Conclude the discussion by having youngsters brainstorm a list of things they should do if they ever become lost.

Midnight Prints

All aboard for midnight prints! In advance, cut several sponges into simple locomotive shapes. Also cut several 1/4" sponge strips of various lengths and several star shapes. To make a print, press a locomotive sponge into white tempera paint, then onto a sheet of black construction paper. Print 1/4" strips to create train tracks and stars to create a nighttime scene. If desired, assist each youngster in writing an outdoor safety rule along the bottom of his paper with white crayon or chalk. To complete the scene, spray the paper lightly with spray fixative or hair spray before dusting it with silver or clear glitter. Display the completed prints on a bulletin board or bind them in a class booklet titled "Choo Choo's Safety Rules."

ERIC CARLE

"Halt! I Have A Story For You!"

Of all the questions children ask Eric Carle, the question he hears most often is "Where do ideas come from?" To Eric, ideas don't come from just one place. They come from a lifetime of experiences—all the thoughts in a person's mind and all the feelings in a person's heart. So Eric likes to answer that question the way his Uncle August did. First he tells the children that they have to wind up his thinking machine. As the children wind an imaginary lever near his temple, Eric makes the whirring thinking-machine noises. After a little while he shouts, "Halt! I have a story for you!" So where do stories come from? According to Eric Carle, "They come from your thinking machine. All you have to do is wind it up!"

Have You Seen My Cat?
Published by Scholastic Inc.

In this story, a little boy goes on a round-the-world quest for his lost cat. Throughout his search, he encounters many members of the cat family—but none of those cats is his cat. At long last, he finds his cat—and a very special surprise awaiting!

Follow up a shared reading of *Have You Seen My Cat?* with this cat-matching activity. Cut out a collection of cat pictures—at least two of each picture. If desired, photocopy the endpapers of the book. Using water-based markers, color the pictures; then cut them out and mount the pictures on construction paper. Give each child a cat picture. Then seat youngsters in a circle and choose one child to be It. Have that child stand in the center of the circle, showing his picture. Then have him ask one classmate at a time, "Have you seen my cat?" If the seated child is holding a different cat picture, he replies by saying, "No, I have not seen your cat." If he is holding a matching picture, he says, "Yes, I have seen your cat!" After showing the matching pictures, choose another child to be It and continue playing in the same manner. Encourage more advanced students to use the actual names of the cats by asking (for example), "Have you seen my jaguar?" Afterwards use the pictures to play a memory game.

Pamela Dionne—Gr. K, Jennifer McDevitt—Gr. K, Londonderry Children's Centre, Londonderry, NH

The Very Quiet Cricket
Published by Philomel Books

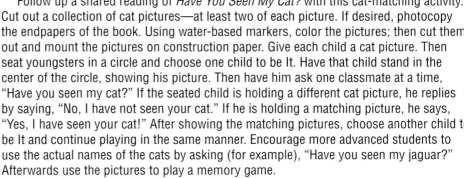

The very quiet cricket journeys through his world meeting one friendly insect after another. He longs to answer his neighbors' cheery greetings, but when he rubs his wings together nothing happens—not a sound. Eventually the cricket meets another cricket who is also a very quiet cricket. Your little ones will be thrilled to actually hear what happens as they turn the last page of the book!

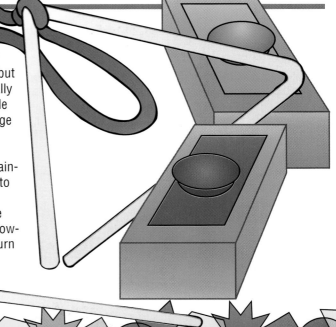

After sharing this intriguing book with your class, choose one child to pretend to be a cricket. Have the cricket hop away and hide while the remaining children close their eyes. At your signal, encourage the hiding cricket to make sounds by doing things such as rubbing two sand blocks together, gently striking a musical triangle, or opening *The Very Quiet Cricket* to the last page. Then choose another student to locate the hiding cricket by following the sounds. Continue in the same manner until each child has had a turn to hide and/or seek. This activity is a wonderful springboard for studying sound and the sense of hearing.

Cathie Pesa—Pre/K, Youngstown City Schools, Youngstown, OH

Rooster's Off To See The World
Published by Picture Book Studio

This selection from the Carle collection is a real winner for children who are ready to begin thinking mathematically. With brilliantly inviting collage illustrations, Eric Carle takes the young reader on a trip with Rooster—who has decided one morning that he'd like to travel! As he travels, Rooster is joined by animal companions who come in sets of two, three, four, and five. Over the course of the story, he is subsequently abandoned by these companions—once again in sets, but this time in descending order.

Prepare this center activity to be used in conjunction with *Rooster's Off To See The World*. You will need ten large, blank index cards. Glue one rooster cutout (or photocopy) on one of the cards, two cat cutouts on another card, three frog cutouts on a third card, and so on. Then label each of the five remaining cards with a different numeral from one to five. Place the prepared cards and a copy of the book in a center. To use this center, a child may match the numerals to the sets, sequence the cards in numerical order, or retell the story using the cards as storytelling pieces.

Tracey Gest—Gr. K, J. Houston Elementary, Austin, TX

Today Is Monday
Illustrated by Eric Carle, Published by Scholastic Inc.

The days of the week, food items, and some pretty interesting animal illustrations are the focus of this humorous book. After reading it aloud to your class, follow the music at the end of the book and learn the story as a song!

After sharing this story and song, have all of your youngsters participate in creating a mural display inspired by *Today Is Monday*. Use an opaque projector to enlarge each of the animals in the book onto bulletin-board paper. Provide paint, glue, feathers, yarn, and other art supplies. Then have small groups of children work together to decorate each animal. Encourage each group to use art supplies and empty food packages to make each animal's respective food choice (according to the book). Mount the completed projects on a bulletin board or wall. Program sentence strips with selected portions of the book's text; then mount them near the appropriate animals. This not only makes an impressive display, but can also be used for visual cuing when retelling the story or singing the song.

Teresa Borrelli—Gr. K, Kate Taugher—Gr. K, St. Alphonsus School, Greendale, WI

Papa, Please Get The Moon For Me
Published by Scholastic Inc.

Against a background of a rich and clear nighttime sky, a little girl asks her father, "Papa, please get the moon for me." As the father sets out to accomplish this task, the reader is fancifully drawn up and into the wondrous sky to experience the moon and its phases.

In advance, gather a collection of colorful photographs of the moon and its phases. Then share the book with your boys and girls. After discussing the story, display the photographs of the moon and introduce vocabulary that is appropriate for your students such as *full moon, half-moon,* and *quarter moon*. For each child, cut out a white construction-paper circle and cut a curved slit in a sheet of black construction paper that matches the diameter of the circle (for example, if you cut an eight-inch circle, cut an eight-inch slit in the black paper). Give each child a circle (moon), black paper (sky), and art supplies such as crayons, chalk, glitter pens, and stick-on stars. Inspired by the story, have each child embellish his moon and sky as desired. When their artwork is complete, encourage children to slide their moons into the slits in the sky to simulate the phases of the moon. These projects can also be used as children tell original moon stories.

Kathleen Dominski—Gr. K, Patterson Elementary, Holly, MI

A House For Hermit Crab
Published by Picture Book Studio

This magnificent underwater tour is a modern-day fable based on the actual habits of the hermit crab. The story not only introduces young readers or viewers to a spectacular marine environment, but also offers a message of hope to young children—and adults—facing the challenges of growing up. As an added bonus, Eric Carle addresses each month of the year in the text.

Continue each child's journey into Hermit Crab's undersea world by having him create a work of art depicting what he thinks Hermit Crab's next home might look like. Display a copy of *A House For Hermit Crab* for student reference. Encourage youngsters to carefully examine the illustrations in the story and on the endpapers. Then provide finger paints, watercolor paints, and wide brushes. Give each child a large sheet of art paper and have him use the supplies as he wishes to create an underwater background. When the paint is dry, have each child add a tissue-paper or construction-paper ocean floor, cut out a construction-paper shell, and glue the shell to his background. Using a permanent marker or construction-paper cutouts, instruct each child to add a hermit crab to the scene. Then have children decorate their shells using felt scraps, glitter, colored glue, pipe cleaners, and other interesting art supplies.

Tarie Curtiss—Gr. K, Arthur Road Early Education Center, Solon, OH

Draw Me A Star
Published by Philomel Books

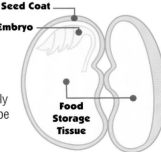

This is a story about an artist—from his earliest drawing years to adulthood. The simple, yet poignant, text can be enjoyed by children and adults alike. With Eric Carle's striking collage illustrations, this book powerfully celebrates and inspires the artist in all of us.

Let your little artists shine by creating these twinkling delights. Have each child use tempera paint to paint a sheet of aluminum foil with a variety of colors and designs. Set the foil aside to dry overnight. Next have each child draw a star design on a sheet of construction paper and cut it out.

When the painted foil is dry, have each child randomly cut his foil into many small pieces, and glue the foil pieces onto his star cutout. After the glue is dry, suspend these twinklers from the ceiling.

Pamela Dionne—Gr. K, Jennifer McDevitt—Gr. K, Londonderry Children's Centre, Londonderry, NH

The Tiny Seed
Published by Picture Book Studio

Eric Carle has created a treasure in this book. Taking us along on the adventures of a tiny seed, this captivating story teaches about seasons and the life cycle of a flower—almost without the readers even knowing it!

Follow up a reading of *The Tiny Seed* with an extension activity involving measurement. Provide assorted colors of construction paper, scissors, and glue. Ask each child to cut or tear the construction paper and assemble a flower similar to those in *The Tiny Seed*. Then mount each flower on a bulletin board or sheet of chart paper. Encourage each child to measure the flowers by using items such as Unifix® cubes, paper clips, clay, or rulers. Provide paper and pencils for those children who wish to record their discoveries.

Ruth Stanfill—Grs. K-1 Special Education, South Roxana School, South Roxana, IL

Exactly what caused that tiny seed to grow in the first place? Pose that question to your little ones; then gather supplies to set up a discovery science center. Soak a supply of lima beans in water overnight. (Soak several more beans than the number of students you have in your class.) Place the soaked beans in a center along with some paper towels and magnifying glasses. As each child visits the center, encourage her to carefully remove the outer covering of a lima bean; then assist her in splitting the seed in half. A small "baby" plant will be visible to the eye, but children may enjoy using magnifying glasses for further exploration.

Carol Komperda—Gr. K, Albany Avenue School, Massapequa Park, NY

Seed Coat

Embryo

Food Storage Tissue

The Grouchy Ladybug
Published by HarperCollins Children's Books

From sunrise to sunset, this little spotted insect challenges everyone and anyone to fight. After a full day of badgering and bullying, the grouchy ladybug finally meets its match in the most unlikely of formidable opponents. *The Grouchy Ladybug* is a valuable classroom book in that it is an ideal literature connection to subjects such as time, insects, and manners. In addition to all that, youngsters are captivated and amused by the story and illustrations.

After sharing aloud *The Grouchy Ladybug*, have your class make this accordion-style big book to reinforce sequencing events and time concepts. Cut 18 large sheets of identically sized poster board. Program each of 17 of the sheets with a clock face showing a different time from the story. Adding the remaining page to the front for a cover, tape all of the pages in chronological order. (Tape them side-by-side so that they will fold accordion-style.) For each of the pages, assign a child (or small group of children) to examine the clock face on the big book page and match it to a clock face from *The Grouchy Ladybug*. Then have him illustrate that particular story event on a separate sheet of art paper. (Also ask one child/group to create illustrations for the title page.) When each child's illustration is complete, have him cut out and glue his illustrations to the appropriate page of the big book. During a group reading time, have youngsters share their pages and retell the story in their own words.

Gerry Porter—Gr. K, St. Aloysius, East Liverpool, OH

Extend the ladybug theme by making ladybug T-shirts. (You can also adapt the process that follows to create ladybug art on other available materials or paper.) In advance, cut various sizes of oval shapes from sponges. If desired, hot-glue an empty thread spool to each sponge for easier handling. Ask each child to bring in a clean T-shirt. To make one ladybug T-shirt, lay a shirt out on a flat surface. Place several layers of flat newspaper inside the shirt so the paint will not bleed through the fabric. Use a brush to paint one side of an oval sponge with fabric paint. Press the sponge onto the shirt to make a print. Repeat the process as often as you like. When the paint is dry, add details with black fabric paint. Have your youngsters sport these designer T-shirts when you're studying related topics.

Carol Komperda—Gr. K, Albany Avenue School, Massapequa, NY

Kids just love concocting these cute confections! Make a batch of sugar cookies (or have a parent donate one cookie for each child plus a few extras). When the cookies are cool, provide red frosting, plastic knives, raisins, chocolate sprinkles, and licorice strands. Have each child frost a cookie, then use the supplies to decorate it to resemble a ladybug. Enjoy these sweet treats together!

Kimberly Calhoun—Pre-K, MacGregor Creative School, Cary, NC

The Very Hungry Caterpillar
Published by Scholastic Inc.

The Very Hungry Caterpillar has quickly become a Carle classic! Young readers love counting with this little caterpillar as he munches his way through the days of the week—to a surprise ending!

Reinforce letter recognition and the hard *C* sound by making these clever caterpillars. Cut out a large supply of construction-paper *C*s. To make a caterpillar body, have each child glue a succession of *C*s onto a long sheet of heavy paper. Encourage each child to design additional caterpillar features using crayons or paint. These creative critters look nice displayed across a long section of your classroom wall.

Carrie Richardson—Gr. K, Betty Horton—Gr. K,
Dr. Samuel A. Mudd Elementary School, Waldorf, MD

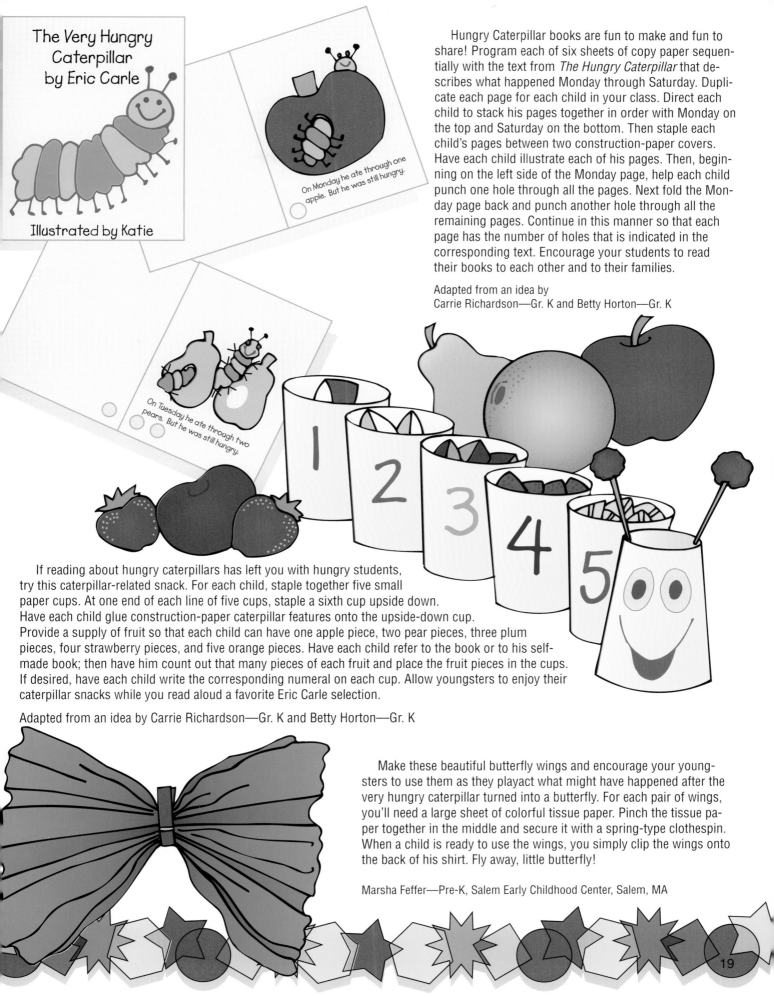

The Very Hungry
Caterpillar
by Eric Carle

Illustrated by Katie

On Monday he ate through one apple. But he was still hungry.

On Tuesday he ate through two pears. But he was still hungry.

Hungry Caterpillar books are fun to make and fun to share! Program each of six sheets of copy paper sequentially with the text from *The Hungry Caterpillar* that describes what happened Monday through Saturday. Duplicate each page for each child in your class. Direct each child to stack his pages together in order with Monday on the top and Saturday on the bottom. Then staple each child's pages between two construction-paper covers. Have each child illustrate each of his pages. Then, beginning on the left side of the Monday page, help each child punch one hole through all the pages. Next fold the Monday page back and punch another hole through all the remaining pages. Continue in this manner so that each page has the number of holes that is indicated in the corresponding text. Encourage your students to read their books to each other and to their families.

Adapted from an idea by
Carrie Richardson—Gr. K and Betty Horton—Gr. K

If reading about hungry caterpillars has left you with hungry students, try this caterpillar-related snack. For each child, staple together five small paper cups. At one end of each line of five cups, staple a sixth cup upside down. Have each child glue construction-paper caterpillar features onto the upside-down cup. Provide a supply of fruit so that each child can have one apple piece, two pear pieces, three plum pieces, four strawberry pieces, and five orange pieces. Have each child refer to the book or to his self-made book; then have him count out that many pieces of each fruit and place the fruit pieces in the cups. If desired, have each child write the corresponding numeral on each cup. Allow youngsters to enjoy their caterpillar snacks while you read aloud a favorite Eric Carle selection.

Adapted from an idea by Carrie Richardson—Gr. K and Betty Horton—Gr. K

Make these beautiful butterfly wings and encourage your youngsters to use them as they playact what might have happened after the very hungry caterpillar turned into a butterfly. For each pair of wings, you'll need a large sheet of colorful tissue paper. Pinch the tissue paper together in the middle and secure it with a spring-type clothespin. When a child is ready to use the wings, you simply clip the wings onto the back of his shirt. Fly away, little butterfly!

Marsha Feffer—Pre-K, Salem Early Childhood Center, Salem, MA

The Very Busy Spider
Published by Scholastic Inc.

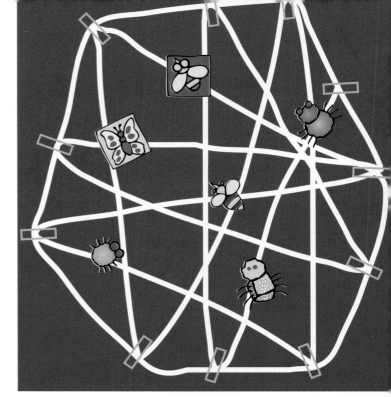

One by one, the little spider's friends come by to entice her away from her work. But the little spider is so busy that she doesn't even answer the "Neigh! Neigh!" of the horse or the "Moo! Moo!" of the cow. Indeed—this spider is *extremely* busy!

Share this story with your busy boys and girls, and they will be intrigued to "spin" and decorate a web of their own. Seat youngsters around a large sheet of bulletin-board paper. Give one child a ball of yarn. Ask him to find the end of the yarn and tape it to the paper in front of him. Then have him roll the ball of yarn to a classmate. Have that child tape the yarn to the paper in front of him, then roll the ball of yarn to another classmate. Continue in this manner until a web appears on the paper. Mount the web onto a bulletin board. Then have children use art supplies—such as egg-carton sections, pompoms, wiggle eyes, and pipe cleaners—to make spiders. After attaching the spiders to the board, have youngsters cut out or draw pictures of insects that a spider might catch and glue them onto the display.

Marsha Feffer—Pre-K, Salem Early Childhood Center, Salem, MA

Cathie Pesa—Pre-K, Youngstown City Schools, Youngstown, OH

"Baa! Baa!" bleated the sheep. "Want to run in the meadow?"

The spider didn't answer. She was very busy spinning her web.

The Very Busy Spider provides a wonderful text for studying textures and the sense of touch. Enlist the help of your students to make this big book. For each event in the story, program a big book page. Then creatively illustrate each of the pages. Make the animals by using different fabrics and materials such as felt, fake fur, wool, feathers, and smooth pieces of rubber. Make the web by squeezing glittery puff paint onto each page. When everything is in place and dry, read the book together. Then keep it available for youngsters to explore in their free time.

Pamela Dionne—Gr. K, Londonderry Children's Centre, Londonderry, NH

This sparkly art project resembles a spiderweb in the early morning dew. Cut black construction-paper circles to fit in the bottom of a round cake pan. Cover the bottom of a shallow pan or dish with white tempera paint. To make a web, place a black circle in the cake pan. Drop a marble into the paint and roll it around until it is coated with paint. Then place the marble on the black circle in the cake pan and shift the pan to roll the marble around. (If more paint is needed, redip the marble.) Before the paint is dry, sprinkle the weblike design with very fine silver glitter. While the web is drying, draw, color, and cut out a spider. When the paint has dried, glue the spider onto the web. Mount the finished project on a sheet of construction paper. Display these glistening webs near your Eric Carle collection.

Judy Pilcher—Gr. K, Russell School, Moscow, ID

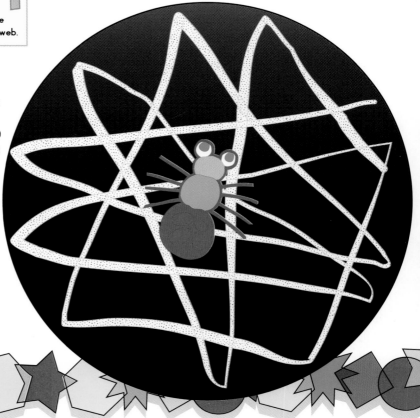

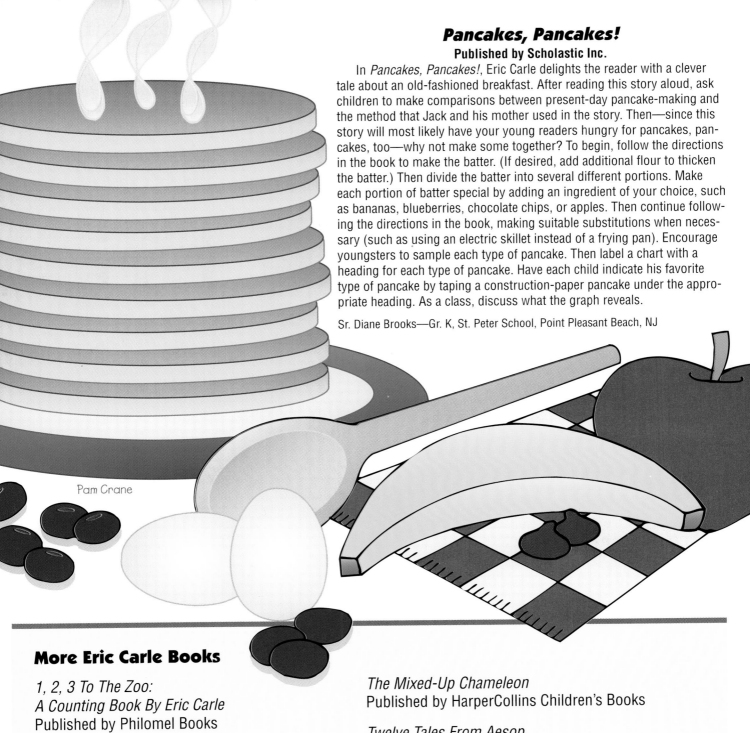

Pancakes, Pancakes!
Published by Scholastic Inc.

In *Pancakes, Pancakes!*, Eric Carle delights the reader with a clever tale about an old-fashioned breakfast. After reading this story aloud, ask children to make comparisons between present-day pancake-making and the method that Jack and his mother used in the story. Then—since this story will most likely have your young readers hungry for pancakes, pancakes, too—why not make some together? To begin, follow the directions in the book to make the batter. (If desired, add additional flour to thicken the batter.) Then divide the batter into several different portions. Make each portion of batter special by adding an ingredient of your choice, such as bananas, blueberries, chocolate chips, or apples. Then continue following the directions in the book, making suitable substitutions when necessary (such as using an electric skillet instead of a frying pan). Encourage youngsters to sample each type of pancake. Then label a chart with a heading for each type of pancake. Have each child indicate his favorite type of pancake by taping a construction-paper pancake under the appropriate heading. As a class, discuss what the graph reveals.

Sr. Diane Brooks—Gr. K, St. Peter School, Point Pleasant Beach, NJ

Pam Crane

More Eric Carle Books

1, 2, 3 To The Zoo:
A Counting Book By Eric Carle
Published by Philomel Books

Do You Want To Be My Friend?
Published by HarperCollins Children's Books

Eric Carle's Animals, Animals
Published by Scholastic Inc.

The Lamb And The Butterfly
Written by Arnold Sundgaard
Illustrated by Eric Carle
Published by Orchard Books

The Mixed-Up Chameleon
Published by HarperCollins Children's Books

Twelve Tales From Aesop
Retold & Illustrated by Eric Carle
Published by Philomel Books

Secret Birthday Message
Published by HarperCollins Children's Books

Dragons Dragons & Other Creatures That Never Were
Published by Putnam Publishing Group

NANCY'S NEIGHBORHOOD

Using Nancy Carlson's Books In Your Classroom

Welcome to the humorous and heartwarming neighborhood created by Nancy Carlson! You and your youngsters will come to know and love Carlson's clever characters. With Nancy Carlson's stories, your little ones will learn to recognize and deal with their own fears, laugh good-naturedly at their own foibles, and cheer for their own successes as well as the successes of others. Enjoy these stories with your boys and girls to help boost self-esteem, encourage the value of family and friendship, and foster a greater acceptance for diversity.

Books About Self-Esteem

I Like Me!
Published by Viking Kestrel

Since children learn best when they feel good about themselves, nurturing positive self-esteem in your students is one of your greatest goals. Nancy Carlson's well-known *I Like Me!* helps you to do just that.

After sharing the book, encourage each child to follow the pig's example and verbalize some of the things that he likes about himself. Ask youngsters to specifically share activities that they enjoy doing alone, ways they take care of themselves, and things they do to cheer themselves up. After your discussion, make a class big book.

In advance, title a large sheet of construction paper "We Like Us!" Program three additional large sheets of construction paper as shown in the illustration, and photocopy a supply of each page. Ask each child to draw a self-portrait on the cover. Then have each child illustrate and write to complete the pages as he desires. Give each child the opportunity to contribute one, two, or three pages to the class book. Bind all of the pages together behind the cover; then have each child share his page(s) with the class during a group reading time.

I can do fun things. I... can tumble around.

I can take care of myself. I... can take a bubble bath.

I can cheer myself up. I... can sing The Little Mermaid.

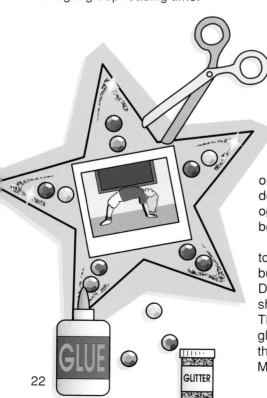

Louanne Pig In The Talent Show
Published by Carolrhoda Books, Inc.

Everyone in Louanne's school is excited about the upcoming talent show. Everyone, that is, except Louanne. Poor Louanne feels that she is "just a big, no-talent dope!" Because there is a little Louanne in each of us, youngsters are likely to recognize and identify with Louanne's insecurities and fears, and cheer her on to become part of the show.

Read the story aloud to your children. After discussing the story, ask each child to think of one thing that he can do well. Ask questions like the following: "Can you build a tall tower? Say or sing all the words to a poem or song? Empty the trash? Do 11 jumping jacks? Count to ten in Spanish?" Then hold an impromptu talent show in your classroom. Take a photograph of each child performing his talent. Then have each child trace and/or cut out a large construction-paper star. Provide glitter, sparkly sequins, and glue for each child to use to decorate his star. When the stars are decorated and dry, glue each child's photo to the center of his star. Mount the stars on a bulletin board titled "We're Loaded With Talent!"

Harriet And The Roller Coaster
Published by Carolrhoda Books, Inc.

Harriet's in line for the big roller coaster—the one that's so big you can't even see the top—and she's feeling a little bit nervous. Well, maybe a *lot* nervous! But George has been taunting her for days about being too scared to ride it. Should Harriet ride the big roller coaster? Your little ones might actually feel some of Harriet's nervous excitement as they get caught up in the rise and fall of this exciting story with a surprise ending.

Read aloud *Harriet And The Roller Coaster,* stopping right after the text reads, "There's still time for you to chicken out." Ask youngsters to share what they think Harriet ought to do at that point. Find out what your youngsters would do if they were in the same situation. Then finish reading the story aloud. Ask each child to tell about a time when he was afraid of something or didn't think he'd like something—but when he tried it, he liked it! Then turn back to the page that shows Harriet worrying in her bed. Ask children what they think Harriet might be thinking and feeling. Then give each child a sheet of construction paper. Have each child draw a picture of himself and write about something that he has worried about (or is currently worrying about). On another sheet of paper, have each child draw the actual outcome (or a possible outcome). Tape the two pages together end-to-end (see the illustration). Have each child fold the outcome picture back so that it is hidden from the class. If appropriate, ask each child to share his page with the class and have his classmates predict what the outcome might be. After the predictions, have the child reveal the outcome.

Families

2	3	4	5	6

Louanne Pig In The Perfect Family
Published by Carolrhoda Books, Inc.

Louanne has a family of three—but she thinks that George's family of ten is the perfect size for a family. Children will laugh, as well as think, when Louanne gets a chance to experience the grass on the other side of the backyard fence!

After sharing the story, encourage children to discuss the advantages and disadvantages of having a large/small family. Then make a graph similar to the one shown. Give each child a construction-paper square and have her draw faces on the paper to represent the number of people in her family. Ask each child to glue her square to the appropriate place on the graph. When each child's family is represented, discuss what the graph reveals.

Harriet & Walt
Published by Carolrhoda Books, Inc.

This selection facilitates a discussion about how family members show that they care for one another. Have each child share ways that he or his family members show they care. Then ask each child to think of something that someone in his family has taught him how to do. Give each child a color copy of the thank-you note on page 25. Have each child write/draw on the note to thank that particular family member for caring about him. Encourage each child to give the note to the appropriate family member and share his or her reaction with the class.

23

Loudmouth George And The New Neighbors
Published by Carolrhoda Books, Inc.

When a family of pigs moves in next door to Loudmouth George, Harriet rushes to George's house so the two of them can go meet the neighbors together. But George will have nothing to do with the pigs next door. He says that pigs are dirty and eat garbage. "They're not like us at all," says George.

Share this story with your youngsters. Brainstorm a list of ways in which George, Louanne, Harriet, and Ralph are the same. Write the ideas on a sheet of chart paper labeled "Friends." Then brainstorm a list of ways in which they are different. After discussing the lists, pair students. Give each student pair a large sheet of construction paper. Encourage each child to talk to his partner to determine commonalities and differences. Then have them write and illustrate one thing they have in common and one thing that is different. Have each student pair share their page with the class. Then bind all the pages between two construction-paper covers labeled "Friends."

Louanne Pig In Making The Team
Published by Carolrhoda Books, Inc.

Louanne wants desperately to make the cheerleading squad. And Arnie wants to be on the football team. It seems, however, that each friend is more skilled at the other's sport! Will their dedication to practice and their encouragement of each other pay off in the end?

Read this book aloud to your youngsters. After discussing the story, divide your class in half. Teach one-half of the class how to make a football craft, while an adult volunteer teaches the other half of the class how to make a pom-pom. (See the directions below.) When the crafts are done, have each child from the football group pair off with a child from the pom-pom group. Encourage children to teach each other how to make their respective crafts. Then display the finished projects on a bulletin board titled "Hooray For Teamwork!"

Football: Have each child trace a football pattern on a double thickness of construction paper, then cut it out. Direct each child to staple the two patterns together, leaving about a three-inch opening. Have each child stuff pieces of tissue paper into the football, then staple it closed. Next have each child glue lengths of yarn onto the football to resemble the football laces.

Pom-pom: Have each child cut many strips of colorful tissue paper or crepe paper. Instruct each child to hold all the strips together and secure the ends with a rubber band. Then assist each child in stapling the banded end to a piece of tagboard. Have each child write his name on the tagboard.

Culminating Activity

Wrap up your study of Nancy Carlson's books with this form of book reporting designed for young children. Assign one child (or a small group of children) to each book that you used in your classroom. Give the child (or group) a large sheet of construction paper. Have him fold the paper in half, and then in half again. Direct him to open the paper and copy the headings as shown on his paper. Then ask each child to refer to his designated book, and illustrate and write to fill in the boxes on the paper. When each child has completed his book report, have him share it with the class. End your Nancy Carlson unit by taking class votes to determine your youngsters' favorite Nancy Carlson book and character.

More Nancy Carlson Books

Arnie And The New Kid
Published by Viking

Harriet's Recital
Published by Carolrhoda Books, Inc.

Harriet And The Garden
Published by Carolrhoda Books, Inc.

Louanne Pig In Witch Lady
Published by Carolrhoda Books, Inc.

Loudmouth George And The Sixth-Grade Bully
Published by Carolrhoda Books, Inc.

Loudmouth George And The Big Race
Published by Carolrhoda Books, Inc.

Loudmouth George And The Fishing Trip
Published by Carolrhoda Books, Inc.

Loudmouth George And The Cornet
Published by Carolrhoda Books, Inc.

A Visit To Grandma's
Published by Viking

What If It Never Stops Raining?
Published by Viking

Thank-You Note   Use with *Harriet & Walt* on page 23.

Nancy White Carlstrom

Nancy White Carlstrom has been a children's librarian, a schoolteacher, and the owner of her own bookstore! After the birth of her first child, she devoted her time to mothering and writing. Nancy White Carlstrom's popular *Jesse Bear, What Will You Wear?* had its origins in a song she sang while dressing her young son. When this story was accepted for publication, Carlstrom had already received 82 rejections on other stories! Thanks to her perseverance and dedication, Nancy White Carlstrom has since published numerous books to the delight of her devoted readers!

Who Gets The Sun Out Of Bed?

Illustrated by David McPhail
Published by Little, Brown And Company

"In the cold, dark winter, who gets the sun out of bed?" Not the spruce tree, nor the fire, nor the wind! So *who* gets the sun out of bed? Explore answers to this question with your youngsters prior to reading *Who Gets The Sun Out Of Bed?* Then, after reading the story aloud, have each child make this lazy sun project. Provide each child with a 12" x 18" sheet of construction paper and an eight-inch-square piece of fabric. To make a bed, have the student glue three edges of the fabric to the paper. Then have him glue pieces of tissue paper onto a construction-paper circle (sized to fit under the fabric square) to create a sun. To put the sun to bed, insert it under the open edge of the fabric. Remove the sun to get it out of bed. On his paper, encourage each child to write or dictate a statement telling who gets the sun out of bed. Display the pictures in your classroom windows.

Carmen Carpenter—Pre-K
Highland Preschool
Raleigh, NC

Ivan gets the sun out of bed.

The Moon Came Too

Illustrated by Stella Ormai
Published by Macmillan Publishing Company
(This book is out of print. Check your library.)

A little girl packs all of her treasures in preparation for a trip to her grandma's house. As she shares her favorite things with her grandma, the girl discovers that a very special treasure has come along too. After reading the story aloud, have students prepare this suitcase filled with some of their favorite things. For each child, cut the ends of a folded sheet of 12" x 18" construction paper to resemble handles on a suitcase. From catalogs and magazines, encourage the child to cut out pictures of some of his favorite things, such as toys, clothes, and nature items. Have him glue the pictures on his suitcase cutout to represent a packed bag. Then have the child cut a moon shape from white construction paper. On his moon, assist him as needed in writing "The moon came too." Attach one end of a length of yarn to the child's moon and the other end to his suitcase handle. Fold the suitcase in half, placing the moon inside. On the outside, have each child write his name. Encourage him to show his family the contents of his suitcase as he tells about the story.

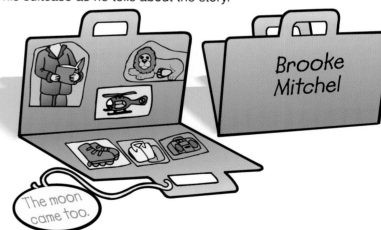

Brooke Mitchel

The moon came too.

Rise And Shine!

Illustrated by Dominic Catalano
Published by HarperCollins Publishers

Invite youngsters to bring to life this delightfully descriptive story about animal activity on a farm. After reading the story aloud, pair students and assign each pair a character from the story (for example, one pair may be roosters and another may be dogs). Then read the story again, this time encouraging each pair of students to listen for its assigned character. When the page with that pair's character is read, have the partners act out the movements and sounds described. For subsequent readings of the story, assign different characters to each pair.

Jesse Bear, What Will You Wear?

Illustrated by Bruce Degen
Published by Simon & Schuster

When asked what he will wear, Jesse Bear has an answer for every occasion. Not only does he wear his clothes; but he also wears his world and experiences. After reading this story, discuss the many things students wear. Include items—other than clothing—that may cover some or all of their bodies, even if only momentarily. For example, suggest that they wear glue during art, bubbles during a bubble-bath, and even a kiss for a very short time!

To extend the discussion, have each student describe the clothes he is wearing. Then provide him with a duplicated sheet of paper programmed with an outline of a bear and "_____ Bear, what will you wear? What will you wear to school? I'll wear my _____ to school." Have the child draw clothing on the bear to resemble his own. Then have him write his name and an article of his clothing on the lines. Place the completed pages between two construction-paper covers, staple them along the left edge, and title the class book "What Will You Wear?" Encourage student partners to read the book together.

Christine Bear, what will you wear? What will you wear to school? I'll wear my red sweater to school.

Diane Billman—Gr. K
Russell School
Smyrna, GA

It's About Time, Jesse Bear: And Other Rhymes

Illustrated by Bruce Degen
Published by Macmillan Publishing Company

These Jesse Bear rhymes make perfect discussion-starters revolving around common childhood experiences. As each rhyme is read aloud, encourage students to tell about their own related experiences. If desired, ask them to dictate additional lines to the verse as you write their responses on chart paper. Then, for an extension activity to "Boxes Are Best," create a play center stocked with a few stuffed bears and a large variety of boxes in different shapes and sizes. In turn, have small groups of children play cooperatively in the center. Encourage them to build some of the items named in the rhyme as well as to make their own creations from the boxes.

Better Not Get Wet, Jesse Bear

Illustrated by Bruce Degen
Published by Macmillan Publishing Company

Youngsters will become immersed in these splashy water stations after hearing this story. In advance, request that parents send swimsuits and towels to school with their children for a day of outdoor water play. On that day, prepare some of these water-activity stations with the suggested materials. Read the story aloud; then have children put on their swimsuits. Rotate small groups of students through each water station. Encourage them to tell about their activities and the materials as they play at each station. With all this water fun, youngsters will be drenched in delight!

- Dishwashing station: a water table, bubble solution, plastic dishes, and cleaning cloths
- Fishing station: a plastic aquarium, colored plastic or foam fish, and fishnets
- Plant-watering station: watering cans, plant sprayers, and real or plastic potted plants
- Birdbath station: a large, shallow dish and plastic or rubber birds
- Mud-puddle station: a tray of dirt, disposable plastic plates for holding the puddles, a pitcher of water, and rubber worms
- Swimming station: a plastic swimming pool, plastic boats, and a float

More From The Carlstrom Collection

Blow Me A Kiss, Miss Lilly
Illustrated by Amy Schwartz
Published by Harper & Row, Publishers

Hooray For Me, Hooray For You, Hooray For Blue: Jesse Bear's Colors
Illustrated by Bruce Degen
Published by Little Simon

How Do You Say It Today, Jesse Bear?
Illustrated by Bruce Degen
Published by MacMillan Books For Young Readers

Happy Birthday, Jesse Bear!
Illustrated by Bruce Degen
Published by MacMillan Books For Young Readers

The Snow Speaks
Illustrated by Jane Dyer
Published by Little, Brown And Company

Wild Wild Sunflower Child Anna
Illustrated by Jerry Pinkney
Published by MacMillan Books For Young Readers

THE CREWS CONNECTION

Donald Crews, the son of a trackman for the railroad, was born in Newark, New Jersey, in 1938, and that is where he grew up. But summer after summer began with a long train trip to Cottondale, Florida, where Crews's grandparents lived. Every summer, from the front porch of his grandparents' house, Donald Crews watched the trains pass. His Caldecott Honor book, *Freight Train*, was inspired by these childhood days when he took special delight in counting the cars of passing freights. *Bigmama's* and *Shortcut* are two of Crews's recent titles that reflect his lifelong interest in trains and give us glimpses into his childhood.

Donald Crews has strong ideas about children and art: "All children like to make marks on paper, from scribbles to coloring books. Encouragement can turn casual markings into controlled drawings, and with still more direction and encouragement, drawings can become meaningful forms of self-expression. Introducing new media and new art forms—painting, sculpture, and collage—can stimulate their desire to express themselves, and they become artists."

Bring out the artistic qualitites in your students with these follow-up activities for Crews's books.

Freight Train

After reading *Freight Train* to your youngsters, have students make this freight train art over a period of several days. To make the train track, trace the upper and lower lines of a sentence strip with a marker. Then draw lines to indicate the railroad ties. To make an engine, a caboose, or a car for the train, start with a 6 1/2" x 4" rectangle of construction paper. Then draw or trace the desired design and cut it out. From two 2-inch squares of black construction paper, cut two wheels. Glue the wheels half on and half off the car. Add other details to the engine, caboose, or car using paints, markers, or paper cutouts. When the four sections of your train are complete (an engine, two cars, and a caboose), glue them to the sentence-strip track.

Ellyn Soypher—Preschool, Goldsmith Early Childhood Education Center Baltimore, MD

School Bus

After reading *School Bus* aloud, ask student volunteers to comment on different pictures from the book. Then sing a few verses of "The Wheels On The Bus." Once everyone is in the same school-bus frame of mind, get them involved in making a creative school bus display like the one on page 30.

Light

(This book is out of print. Check your library.)

After reading aloud *Light*, turn on the creativity within each of your youngsters. Discuss lights that they've admired, and lead students in reexamining the illustrations in Crews's book. Point out that sometimes lots of rectangular lights were shown together, sometimes small round lights were shown, and sometimes there was a mixture. Then provide each student with a black sheet of construction paper, a generous supply of the round holes that paper hole punchers make, lots of small square and retangular pieces of paper, and glue. Ask each student to use the supplies to make designs representing lights they've seen or lights they can imagine. When the projects are done, have volunteers tell about their "light-scapes."

Carousel

After reading aloud *Carousel*, have each student make a carousel horse. To make a horse, begin by tracing a large template onto 12" x 18" art paper. Flip the template so that the horse is facing the other way and trace it again on another large sheet of art paper. Paint both horse outlines to resemble carousel horses. When the artwork is dry, cut the horses out and place them back-to-back, wedging a painted gift-wrap tube between them. Secure the cutouts to each other and to the tube with staples or glue. Attach crepe-paper streamers to the top of the tube. When each youngster has prepared one of these carousel horses, play some calliope or circus music as students "mount" their carousel horses and move around in a circle. Have students start out by making their horses go up and down slowly, gradually increasing speed. Later have them gradually slow their pace and the vertical movement of the horses until they come to a stop.

Use Hula-Hoops to create canopies from which to hang your youngsters' carousel horses. Cut four pieces of cord, each about three-fourths the length of the Hula-Hoop's diameter. Holding one end of each cord, make a knot to secure the pieces together. Tie the loose ends to the Hula-Hoop. Use additional cord to suspend the hoop from the ceiling by the original knot. Attach a scalloped length of butcher paper to the hoop. Cut a circle from bulletin-board paper that is about six inches wider than the diameter of the Hula-Hoop. Cut a slit to the center of the circle. Drape the circle over the four cords that hold the Hula-Hoop level. Secure the paper circle to complete the canopy before attaching students' carousel horses to the hoop.

Sheli Gossett, Avon Elementary School, Avon Park, FL

Parade

Read *Parade* to your youngsters. Then give students opportunities to tell about parades that they've attended. Find out what parts of the parades they enjoyed the most. Ask students what preparations different people probably have to make to get ready for a parade. Once everyone's thinking, announce that you're going to have an impromptu class parade. Have each student decide what role he will play in the parade. Some students may want to be clowns or horseback riders, while others may choose to be musicians. Play appropriate march music as youngsters, armed with a few props, march around the classroom or playground.

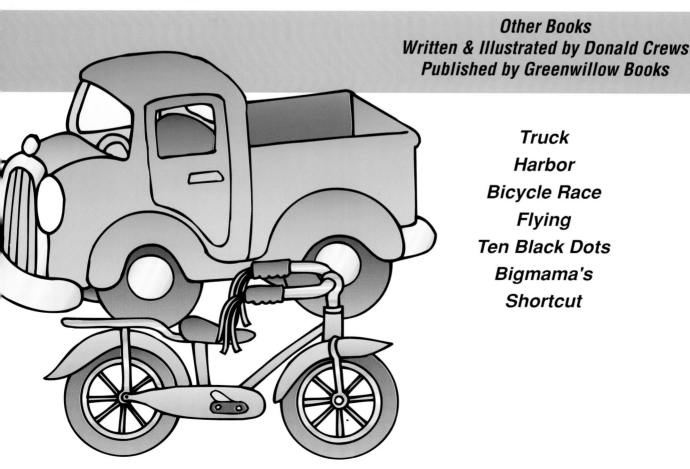

Other Books
Written & Illustrated by Donald Crews
Published by Greenwillow Books

Truck

Harbor

Bicycle Race

Flying

Ten Black Dots

Bigmama's

Shortcut

Cake Pattern

Use with *A Perfect Father's Day* on page 10.

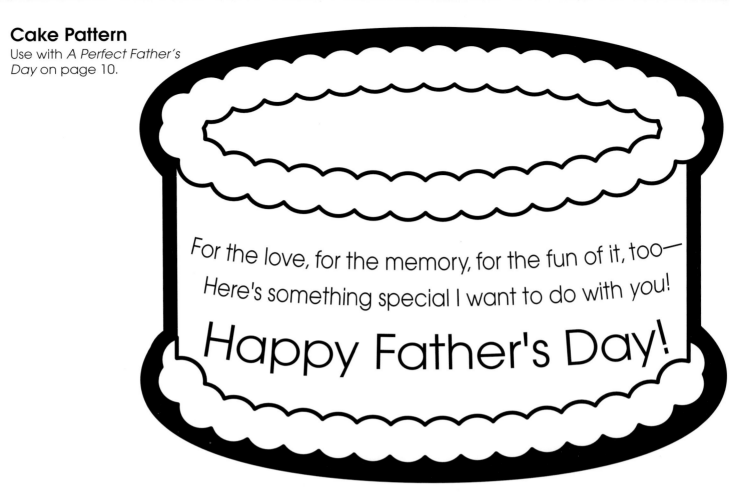

For the love, for the memory, for the fun of it, too—
Here's something special I want to do with you!

Happy Father's Day!

Extend that catchy "Bus Song" into a language arts activity! Mount a large bus cutout on a board. Have children color and cut out illustrations of people or things to be mounted in or on the bus. Write each youngster's dictation on a construction-paper speech balloon; then display it near his illustration. You're sure to hear compliments on this board "all around the school."

Tomie dePaola
Once A Reluctant Kindergartner, Now A Kindergarten Favorite

The day I had been waiting for for a year and a half had arrived. I was finally old enough to go to school. I was so happy and insisted on walking the last block by myself and going alone into the school building. All around me were crying children clinging to their mothers (little did I know that I would share classrooms with these same children for thirteen years!), but not me! I went directly to the lady standing there (who I found out shortly was the principal) and asked where the kindergarten room was, please. Poor Miss Imick, the kindergarten teacher. After introducing myself to her, I immediately confronted her with "When do we learn how to READ?" "Oh," she replied, "we don't learn how to read in kindergarten, we learn how to read next year." "All right," I announced, "I'll be back next year," and promptly walked out the forbidden front door and trudged all the way home. The school telephoned my mother. The police were called, my father rushed home from the barbershop where he worked. I was calmly sitting up in the attic "reading" one of my mother's slightly racy novels—upside down.

Tomie dePaola

Reprinted with permission from *Children's Literature In The Reading Program*, edited by Bernice E. Cullinan, copyright 1987 by the International Reading Association, Inc.

Like his first kindergarten encounter, each of Tomie dePaola's books is refreshingly unique. So choose your favorites from this early childhood sampler of books authored and illustrated by dePaola. Then introduce your youngsters to the reluctant kindergartner who became a prolific writer and illustrator.

From HEY DIDDLE DIDDLE & OTHER MOTHER GOOSE RHYMES by Tomie dePaola, copyright ©1985 and 1988 by Tomie dePaola. Reprinted by permission of Penguin Putnam Books For Young Readers.

The Art Lesson

Published by G. P. Putnam's Sons

You can never be sure how many dePaolas are sitting in your classroom, but you can be certain this story will strike an inspiring chord with all of your little ones. Since this book is somewhat autobiographical, it's a good choice as your first dePaola selection. Explain to your youngsters that the author and the book character have several things in common, such as: a dad who was a barber, Irish grandparents, an Italian grandmother, an art teacher named Beulah Bowers, and the desire to be a REAL artist. Have students closely examine the pictures on the last page. As you are reading other dePaola books, encourage students to identify any characters shown on this page.

Follow up this book by having each youngster draw a picture or two onto art paper using fabric crayons. Following the instructions on the fabric crayon package, transfer each student's favorite design onto a white dishcloth. Students may elect to give these cloths as gifts or to use them when helping with household chores.

"Charlie Needs A Cloak"

Published by Simon & Schuster Books for Young Readers

After he learned how to spin wool and weave, dePaola wrote this story about the making of a shepherd's new cloak. Read aloud the story; then have youngsters examine each illustration to identify the antics of the dark-faced sheep and the sneaky mouse. Ask students to recall the steps of cloak-making. Using simple sketches like those on the last page of the book, make a set of sequential cards so that students can practice ordering the events.

To make a likeness of Charlie, sponge paint the back side of a six-inch paper plate using flesh-colored paint. When dry, decorate it to resemble Charlie's face using markers and a clump of shredded, crumpled, brown tissue paper. Cut Charlie's hat from a 9 1/2" unbleached coffee filter. Use cranberry juice to dye a 12" square of red tissue paper. Attach the hat, face, and dried cloth (or tissue paper) to a 12" x 18" tagboard sheet as shown.

More dePaola Delights

Haircuts For The Woolseys

Published by G. P. Putnam's Sons

For the barber's son who authored *Charlie Needs A Cloak*, *Haircuts For The Woolseys* must have been a snip, snip, snap! After reading aloud *Haircuts For The Woolseys*, have youngsters describe both winter and spring, and ask youngsters to scan the illustrations to identify a character from another dePaola tale (Charlie).

After hearing this story, have each youngster make a "woolsey" of his own. Have each student trace his hand and cut on the outline, before gluing cotton batting to the palm area of the cutout. To complete the effect, attach a wiggle-eye to the thumb area and glue on a tissue-paper kerchief.

Pancakes For Breakfast

Published by Harcourt Brace Jovanovich

Today's youngsters, accustomed to supermarket and fast-food fare, may be surprised to realize just how hard it can be to round up the ingredients for pancakes. When "reading" this story with your youngsters, pause when the lady is on the way back with syrup, and ask youngsters what will happen next. Turn the page and have students comment on the destruction by the pets as well as the lady's pancake prognosis. Then finish the story.

Using the book's recipe, have students prepare pancakes. While they're feasting on these flapjacks, have youngsters contrast their pancake-making experience to that of the lady in the story.

Too Many Hopkins

Published by G. P. Putnam's Sons
(This book is out of print. Check your library.)

After reading this story to your brood, convert an area of your classroom (or the playground) into a "garden" for dramatic play. Display a collection of children's garden tools including a watering can and a wheelbarrow. Have each youngster make a row marker by gluing a flower or vegetable picture to a small tagboard rectangle which has been glued to a tongue depressor. With the inspiration of *Too Many Hopkins* to get them started, youngsters can take turns using this equipment to plant and label a "garden" in a sandbox or sand-filled wading pool.

Andy (That's My Name)

Published by Aladdin Paperbacks

Encourage load after load of word-making fun with *Andy*. Read aloud *Andy*, stopping to examine each word that shows up in Andy's wagon. Then provide a small wagon and letter blocks or a flannel board, flannel-board wagon cutout, and felt letters for students to manipulate. Starting with the word *Andy* in the wagon, just as in the story, have students add and remove letters to make other words. On each of several subsequent days, feature a different student's name in the wagon. Encourage youngsters to remove and add letters to make new words. Each youngster will be tickled pink to have his name featured in the wagon.

Flicks

Published by Harcourt Brace Jovanovich

This nearly wordless book of five "silent movies" is a wonderful introduction to picture-sequencing activities. As you show each picture, have youngsters describe the action. At the end of each picture story sequence, ask your students for their reactions. Are they surprised, for example, that the new baby turned out to be a pet?

Create original flick booklets starring your classroom cast. Photograph the sequence of events as your youngsters complete any classroom project or task. Mount each photograph onto a sheet of construction paper decorated with a duplicated "audience" border (similar to the one in *Flicks*). Similarly prepare a title page. Punch holes in the left margin of each sheet, sequence the sheets, and bind the pages together in a notebook. After "reading" the booklet in the proper sequence, have each student open the rings, mix up the sheets, sequence the pictures, and reassemble the sheets in order.

Oliver Button Is A Sissy

Published by Harcourt Brace Jovanovich
As a first grader, Tomie dePaola took tap lessons at Miss Leah Grossman's Dancing School. Like Oliver, he spent a lot of time reading and drawing and was never asked to play on ball teams, since he lacked athletic ability. Perhaps some of your youngsters can relate to Oliver's and Tomie's problem of just not fitting in. After reading aloud the story, discuss with your students the values of each of their individual talents. Then conduct an informal classroom talent show or exhibit.

Invite each of your youngsters to write a bit of positive graffiti relating to the talents of a classmate. Cover a bulletin board with brick-look Con-Tact paper. Have each youngster draw a classmate's name from a hat. Then assist him as he uses a permanent marker to write something about the talent(s) of the corresponding student on the bulletin board.

The Popcorn Book

Published by Holiday House
Pair this book with a popcorn party and you'll have an all-time favorite on your hands. There's lots to learn—including history and science—between these covers. So read the story aloud; then make popcorn using a recipe from the book.

As the students are munching on mouthfuls of popcorn, have them recall the midwestern drought story from the book. Then list (as students brainstorm) several unusual locations and heat sources. Have each student take a turn specifying a location and a heat source and telling a popcorn tall tale using these elements. Have you heard the one about the nervous schoolhouse mouse who stashed popcorn kernels under the radiator?

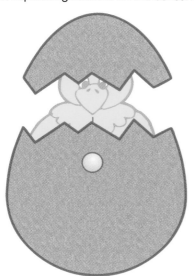

Little Grunt And The Big Egg

Published by Holiday House
Little Grunt had big pet problems. After reading the book aloud, ask each youngster to think of an animal—other than a dinosaur—that could have hatched from the egg. In preparation for this activity, gather one 12" x 18" tagboard sheet and one 12" x 18" pastel, construction-paper sheet for each project, and cut a two-piece, egg-shaped tracer from a 12" x 18" sheet of tagboard. To make a hatchling, draw and color a creature on tagboard, before cutting it out. Trace the egg pieces onto the construction-paper sheet and cut them out. Then glue the smaller eggshell cutout to the hatchling's head. Use an X-acto knife to cut a slit nearly the entire length of the hatchling. Place the other egg cutout atop the hatchling so it matches the portion already glued in place. Insert a brad through the egg cutout and the hatchling's slit. The lower part of the egg can then be slid down to reveal more of the hatchling. Display these projects on a bulletin board titled "What's Hatching?"

The Knight And The Dragon

Published by G. P. Putnam's Sons
Hear ye! Hear ye! This nearly wordless medieval tale trumpets the message that fruitful relationships can be built—even where animosity once existed. As students reexamine the pages showing the result of the fight, have them tell how the dragon and the knight must have felt. Then have students reexamine the barbecue stand scene and again tell how the pair must have felt.

Have youngsters brainstorm other enemy pairs. Then ask youngsters to discuss imaginative ways that these pairs could combine their talents to benefit themselves and those around them. Have youngsters illustrate these new collaborations on bright paper banners.

Got A Minute?— Grab A dePaola

Keep these three dePaola collections at your fingertips, and you'll never be at a loss during transition times.

Tomie dePaola's Favorite Nursery Tales
Tomie dePaola's Book Of Poems
Tomie dePaola's Mother Goose

Introducing... LOIS EHLERT!

As far back as Lois Ehlert can recall, her parents always seemed to be making things. Her dad did some woodworking in a basement workshop, and her mother was an accomplished seamstress. To Lois's delight her parents set up a card table to be her very own working area. Long before Lois Ehlert became a renowned artist/author, she worked at that little card table creating works of art using scrap lumber and nails given to her by her father and fabric scraps contributed by her mother. To this day, Lois Ehlert still sometimes uses that very same card table.

Although Lois did a lot of painting and drawing as she was growing up, her favorite art technique is *collage*—cut-out pieces of paper or fabric glued to a backing. Some of her more recent works of art are featured in this unit. Use your choice of books by Lois Ehlert with the activities suggested, and you'll find that her books help you to unveil fascinating information, create a sense of wonder, and unlock the creativity within your youngsters.

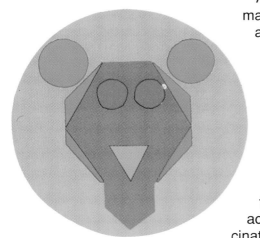

It's Nice To Meet You

One good way for your youngsters to get to know Lois Ehlert and her work is by watching the video entitled *Get To Know Lois Ehlert* (published by Harcourt Brace & Company). This 20-minute video introduces children to Lois's childhood and things in her life that have inspired her books. Children can also see how Lois starts with a model—such as her sister's cat or fresh fruit from the market—and creates a work of art that bears a striking resemblance to the model. This videotape, which retails for $39.95, may be ordered from your local bookstore or by calling Harcourt Brace customer service at 1-800-543-1918.

Circus
Published by HarperCollins

Beautiful antique circus wagons inspired Lois Ehlert to write and illustrate Circus. Prepare your little ones for this story by asking them to share their own circus experiences; then read the book aloud. After discussing the story, show the pictures again, asking each child to volunteer to play one of the book's characters. (Depending on your class size, you might decide to combine or expand parts that contain more than one character, such as the Pretzel brothers or the flying Zucchinis.) After each child has a part, reread the book, directing each child to take note of his assigned character. Then play circus music while each child uses colorful art supplies to make a puppet, mask, or costume to resemble his character. Then—as the ringmaster speaking with the appropriate fanfare—read the text as each child reenacts his part, embellishing the role as he wishes. At the end of the show, announce the characters one at a time so that each actor can come forward to receive a round of applause!

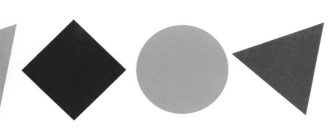

Feathers For Lunch

Published by
Harcourt Brace Jovanovich

Youngsters might giggle, grin, or gasp—but they will all delight in this spirited backyard romp. After reading and discussing *Feathers For Lunch,* revisit the pictures in the book, paying particular attention to each of the birds. Lois Ehlert went to great lengths to be sure that each bird in the story is accurately shown as life-size. Ask youngsters to describe each of the birds and attempt to imitate its song or sound. Then enlarge and reproduce the bird checklist on the back flap. Show youngsters the list and tell them that, as a class, you'd like to see how many of the birds you can spot. Brainstorm ways you might be able to attract birds to an area where they can be seen.

Then have each child make a bird feeder by spreading peanut butter on one side of a rice cake. Cover the bottom of a shallow pan with an inch or two of birdseed. Press each rice cake into the birdseed; then carefully poke a pipe cleaner through the approximate center of each rice cake. Have each child find a place outdoors on which to hang his bird feeder. (It would be great if you could see the feeders from your classroom windows!) When youngsters observe birds, help them identify the types of birds they see and check them off the list.

Color Zoo Color Farm

Published by
HarperCollins

Prior to sharing these two books with your students, cut out a wide variety of colorful construction-paper shapes and shape stencils. Then share *Color Zoo* with your youngsters. Discuss each of the animals, colors, and shapes in the book. At another sitting, read aloud and discuss *Color Farm.* Afterwards title one sheet of chart paper "Zoo Animals" and another sheet "Farm Animals." Then have youngsters brainstorm animals in each category. Encourage youngsters to name animals from each of the books, as well as additional animals they can think of. Also ask youngsters if any of the animals mentioned could go in both categories. (For example, a mouse might be found on a farm as well as at the zoo.) Then make farm and zoo murals by attaching a long sheet of bulletin-board paper to a wall (at students' eye level). Label one half "Zoo" and the other half "Farm." Encourage each child to arrange and glue the construction-paper shapes together or to a background to make farm and/or zoo animals. Have each child attach his animals under the appropriate headings on the mural. When your mural is finished, perhaps you'd like to have another class tour your marvelous menagerie!

Growing Vegetable Soup

Published by
Harcourt Brace Jovanovich

One of Lois Ehlert's continuing pleasures in life is gardening. While you may not be able to actually *grow* vegetable soup in the middle of winter where you live, wouldn't it be wonderful to eat some? Prepare a basket containing the ingredients listed on the recipe card in this illustration. After sharing *Growing Vegetable Soup* with your little ones, read it again and have youngsters pantomime the text. When you get to the page that says, "...and cut them and put them in a pot of water," reveal the stocked basket and a Crock-Pot®. Then enlist the help of your youngsters in following the recipe to make some delicious vegetable soup. Mmmm—soup's on!

Vegetable Soup

1 can green beans
1 can peas
1 can carrots

1 can corn
1 large can crushed tomatoes
1 small onion, diced

Drain the green beans, peas, carrots, and corn. Combine all ingredients in a Crock-Pot®. Simmer until thoroughly heated.

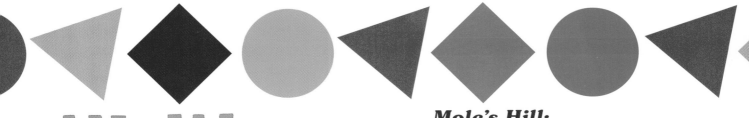

Mole's Hill:
A Woodland Tale
Published by Harcourt Brace & Company

This touching tale sets the perfect stage to get your little ones thinking and talking about conflict resolution. Prior to reading the story, ask students to share times when they have felt bullied or have had disagreements with friends or siblings. Guide students in discussing if and how their conflicts were resolved. Then read aloud *Mole's Hill.* Pause after the text that reads, "Mole went home. She didn't want to move. She loved her home right where it was." Encourage youngsters to think about how each of the characters involved might be feeling. Ask youngsters to offer possible solutions to the problems. Then finish reading the story aloud. Afterward ask students what they think about the story's ending. Then have each child illustrate a page to show what he would do if he were in one of the character's predicaments. Record each child's dictation at the bottom of his page. Compile all of the pages into a book entitled "What Would You Do?" Have each child share his page during a group time.

Fish Eyes:
A Book You Can Count On
Published by Harcourt Brace Jovanovich

There's a whole school of ideas just jumping out of this brilliantly illustrated tale!

Swim It Out!

Read this book aloud to students to introduce or reinforce addition and subtraction concepts. After sharing the book one time, have groups of students act out—or *swim out*—the story as you read the text again. After the guide fish says, "Good-bye!", improvise a subtraction version of the story by having youngsters follow your cues. For example, you could say, "Ten darting fish. Ten darting fish minus one makes nine." Continue the story until there are zero fish remaining.

If You Could Truly Have A Wish,...

Use Lois Ehlert's question at the end of the book to lead children into some fanciful creative writing. Ask youngsters, "If you could truly have a wish, would you wish to be a fish?" Give each child a large sheet of art paper and ask her to illustrate a response to this question. Record each child's dictation on her page and compile all of the pages into a construction-paper big book cover. Have each child share her page during a group time.

Are You For Real?

Swim across the curriculum into science by having each child compare the illustrations in *Fish Eyes* to realistic fish pictures or actual fish in an aquarium. If youngsters look very carefully, they just might find that some of the author's illustrations look very much like real types of fish such as triggerfish, angelfish, rainbow trout, catfish, and guppies.

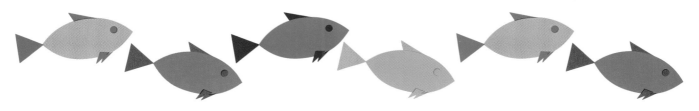

Eating The Alphabet:
Fruits And Vegetables From A To Z
Published by Harcourt Brace Jovanovich

This book is not only a beautiful work of art, but also quite a taste-bud tempter! After sharing *Eating The Alphabet,* tell youngsters that Lois Ehlert used watercolor collages to illustrate this book. For example, Lois cut out each kernel of the Indian corn separately! Have each of your little ones use the same art technique to illustrate a fruit or vegetable. Ask each child to choose a letter of the alphabet and a corresponding fruit or vegetable. Then have him use watercolor paints to paint a page (or pages) of paper with the color (or colors) of his fruit or vegetable. When the paint is dry, have each child cut out shapes from the painted page(s) and glue them together to resemble his chosen fruit or vegetable. Next program a long strip of bulletin-board paper with the letters of the alphabet, being sure to leave ample space between each letter. Direct each child to glue his creation near the appropriate letter on the alphabet strip. Mount the finished project on your classroom wall.

If you've worked up an appetite from all these taste-tempting illustrations, seize the teachable moment! Divide your class into two equal groups. Ask each child in one group to bring in a vegetable of his choice. Ask each child in the second group to bring in a fruit of his choice. (You might consider bringing in some salad dressings or dips.) Encourage each child to learn the name and beginning letter of the food item he brings. After each child "shows and tells" his item, have youngsters cooperatively make one big fruit salad and one big vegetable salad. What a feast!

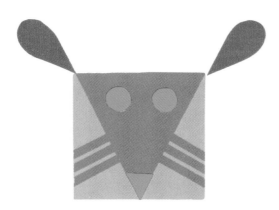

Illustrations from COLOR ZOO by Lois Ehlert. Copyright ©1989 by Lois Ehlert. Used by permission of HarperCollins Publishers.

Planting A Rainbow
Published by Harcourt Brace Jovanovich

Take your youngsters on a journey through the seasons with this colorful story about flower gardening. First ask students if they have ever planted or tended flowers, and encourage them to share their experiences with the class. Then read and discuss *Planting A Rainbow.* Next visually divide a bulletin board into four vertical sections. Label the sections (from left to right) "Fall," "Winter," "Spring," and "Summer." Divide your class into three groups and have each group follow Lois Ehlert's lead in making construction-paper collage pictures to depict what happened in the story during the fall, winter, or spring. Mount the pictures on the board in their respective sections. Then have each child make her own construction-paper flower. Mount all of the flowers in the "Summer" section to create an eye-catching flower rainbow. Just beautiful!

More Lois Ehlert Books

Moon Rope
Published by Harcourt Brace Jovanovich

Nuts To You!
Published by Harcourt Brace Jovanovich

Red Leaf, Yellow Leaf
Published by Harcourt Brace Jovanovich

Denise Fleming!
Using Denise Fleming's Books In Your Classroom

When you introduce children to a book by Denise Fleming, you're presenting a treat for the eyes *and* the ears. Denise Fleming's books take the reader on a joyous romp through color and concepts. Whether it's a nature lesson, a counting experience, or an introduction to wildlife and seasons, Denise Fleming has created an exhilarating collection of books that beckon to be read aloud.

Photograph by David Powers

Illustration from *In the Tall, Tall Grass* copyright ©1991 by Denise Fleming. By permission of Henry Holt & Company.

In The Tall, Tall Grass
Published by Henry Holt And Company

With only a glance, Denise Fleming's bold, bright illustrations draw the reader into this outstanding nature tale. Crawl through the grass with a little caterpillar on a day's journey from sunlight to moonlight. There's a whole world to be discovered—in the tall, tall grass!

After sharing and discussing *In The Tall, Tall Grass,* youngsters will be primed to make these colorful, larger-than-life illustrations. Give each group of four or five students a large sheet of blue butcher paper (about 36" x 36"), a variety of colorful construction paper, and glue. Inspire youngsters to remember what kinds of things the caterpillar saw—or imagine what he might have seen—in the tall, tall grass. Then encourage each child in the group to tear and glue to create a minimural. Display each group's finished project along a wall with the title *"In The Tall, Tall Grass."*

Diane Bonica and Kathy Devlin—Gr. K
Charles F. Tigard School, Tigard, OR

Little hands will be immersed in the tall, tall grass with this story extension. In advance, cut a strip of tagboard that measures 2" x 6" for each child. Use a craft knife to cut two small finger holes at the bottom of each strip. Also fringe-cut enough green construction paper to tape to a table edge or bookcase to resemble grass. Then give each child one prepared tagboard strip, and provide a supply of construction paper, crayons, scissors, and glue. Encourage each child to use the art supplies to create a character from *In The Tall, Tall Grass.* Then have each child make a finger puppet by gluing his creature to his tagboard strip, leaving the holes open at the bottom of the strip. As you reread the book's text aloud, have children creep the appropriate characters through the tall, tall grass.

Andrea M. Troisi—Gr. K
La Salle Middle School
Niagara Falls, NY

Environmental studies, rhyming, and creativity all go into the making of this big book. As a class, brainstorm a list of environments around your school. Then "Fleming-ize" each of the listed environments. For example, you might write "In The Busy, Busy City" or "In The Big, Big Field." Then encourage each child to choose one of the environments and to write/dictate text and illustrate a creature(s) or object(s) that might be found in that particular environment. When each page is complete, have children sort their pictures into categories. Bind each category's pages between construction-paper covers; then have each child share her page with the class.

Sheri Dressler—Gr. K
Woodland School, Carpentersville, IL

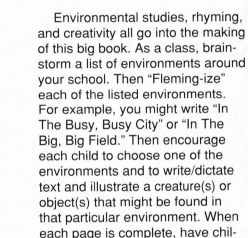

In the Busy, Busy City
by Ms. Dressler's Kindergarten

In the Big, Big Field
by Ms. Dressler's Kindergarten

Vroom, Vroom Cars zoom.

Barry Slate

39

Lunch
Published by Henry Holt and Company, Inc.

This "lunch" is packed with a little, gray mouse who eats his way through an array of colorful fruits and vegetables—and a side order of rich vocabulary words! Just a few bites of this book can reinforce a variety of skills in your hungry learners.

Illustration from *Lunch* copyright ©1992 by Denise Fleming. By permission of Henry Holt & Company, Inc.

After reading and discussing the book with your children, give each child an opportunity to really *indulge* himself in the story! In advance color and/or cut out a picture to represent each of the foods in the book—a turnip, carrots, corn, peas, blueberries, grapes, apples, and watermelon. Mount each picture on a similarly shaped, construction-paper background; then laminate the pictures. Attach a loop of masking tape to the back of each picture. Then use face paint to paint a nose and whiskers on each child. Alternating between groups of eight children, give each child in the group a picture. As you read the text, have each child act out the part that corresponds with the picture he is holding. When each actor's respective part is over, have him press his picture onto his tummy. When the text reads "...he took a nap until...," direct each child to act the part. When you say, "...dinnertime!", have each child crawl off the stage, sniffing for dinner.

Patricia Moeser
University of Wisconsin-Madison
    Preschool Laboratory
Madison, WI

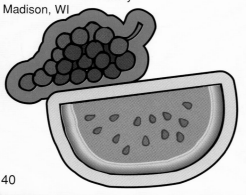

It's only natural that after lunch comes...dinner! So extend the story by writing a sequel entitled *Dinner*. Begin by recalling the types of foods that the mouse ate in *Lunch*. Guide children to determine that the mouse ate vegetables and fruits. Then encourage youngsters to brainstorm a list of foods that the mouse could eat for dinner. Assign each child (or small group of children) one of the foods listed; then encourage him to write/dictate text for and illustrate his page, being sure to include a mouse. Here's the tricky part: When each page is complete, decide on the order in which the mouse will eat the foods. Then challenge each child to color a spot on his mouse to represent the food(s) that the mouse has eaten before he gets to the child's particular food item. (Physically arranging children in sequence helps with this step.) Then bind the pages in order between illustrated construction-paper covers. Have each author/artist share his page during a group reading time.

Joyce Johnson—Gr. K
Bayshore Elementary
Bradenton, FL

He ate curly, red spaghetti.

soft, white bread.

crunchy, brown peanuts.

With this activity, you'll be munching into math served on a bed of rich language development. Ask each child to bring in an uncut fruit or vegetable from home. On a table or countertop, graph the foods; then discuss the results. Also brainstorm additional ways of sorting the foods (such as by color, size, or shape); then do so. Afterward have each child draw and cut out a picture of the food item that he brought in. Glue each picture/group of pictures on a sheet of chart paper. Then wash and cut up each food item. As children sample each food, encourage them to call out words that describe each food. Write the words next to the respective picture on the chart paper. Follow up this tasting event by gluing a large mouse cutout to a sheet of poster board. In turn, have each child paint on a spot of color to represent his food item. Label the cutout similarly to the picture of the mouse on the last page of *Lunch*. Display the poster in your classroom.

Jennifer Strathdee
Palmer Elementary
Baldwinsville, NY

celery	apples	tomatoes	carrots	onions

Barnyard Banter
Published by Henry Holt And Company, Inc.

This exuberant picture book is bursting with so much color, texture, and playful sound that even the most urban dwellers will feel as if they've been down on the farm for a spell. Denise Fleming has created a barnyard masterpiece!

Illustration from *Barnyard Banter* copyright ©1994 by Denise Fleming. By permission of Henry Holt & Company, Inc.

In *Barnyard Banter*, youngsters are introduced to sound words that might be just a little bit different than the sound words they have heard before. After sharing the book, reinforce this new vocabulary by singing the traditional "Old MacDonald" with the sound words from the book. Afterward isolate each of the sound words and discuss the rhyming pairs.

Carmen Carpenter—Pre-K
Highland Preschool, Raleigh, NC

Puzzles! Puzzles!

Your young puzzlers can honk, oink, and moo right along with the engaging *Barnyard Banter* Puzzle For Beginners. Then leap over to a seasonal tour with the big, shaped floor puzzle inspired by *In The Small, Small Pond*. Both of these lively puzzles are available from Briarpatch™ by calling 1-800-232-7427.

Challenge your students to recall one character from the book that is on every page (except one), but never makes a sound. (Revisit the illustrations if necessary.) After children discover the yellow butterfly, encourage them to use position words to describe the butterfly's location on each page. For several consecutive mornings afterward, position a construction-paper butterfly in a different place in your room. When you gather for group time each day, ask who has located the butterfly and encourage children to use position words to guide you to the butterfly.

Jennifer Strathdee, Palmer Elementary, Baldwinsville, NY

This activity brings lots of barnyard noises, as well as emergent reading skills to your classroom. Cut out two tagboard cards for each talkative animal in the story. On one of each pair of cards, glue a cut-out picture of the animal. On the other card in each pair, write the corresponding sound word. (If you have an odd number of children in your class, make more than one card of any given sound to ensure that each child will have a card.) To begin, give each child a card. At your signal, have the children with sound cards make their sounds. Then encourage the children with picture cards to find their matches. When each card has been matched, mix up the cards and play another round. Ready, set,…let the barnyard banter begin!

Patty Welsh Cox—Gr. K
Austin Elementary School, Abilene, TX

Other Books By Denise Fleming

Count!
Published by Henry Holt And Company

Where Once There Was A Wood
Published by Henry Holt And Company

Falling For *Freeman* Books

Since everyone loves *Corduroy*, we've filled this Don Freeman unit with a large supply of follow-up activities tailor-made to use with the *Corduroy* stories. But we've packed the unit with activities related to other fine Freeman titles too. Read through these classroom-tested suggestions and you'll soon be convinced that it will be a lot of fun getting your little ones to fall for Freeman books.

Two very special gifts played powerful roles in Don Freeman's destiny. When he was ten, Don Freeman's dad gave him a shiny brass trumpet for Christmas. Don became a self-taught musician by imitating the recordings he played on a Victrola. Then, in the late 1920s, at the time of his high school graduation, his grandmother gave him a summer course in art at the San Diego School of Fine Arts. In the years to come, Don would often wonder which of these gifts was the most important to him. But in the early 1930s he lost his beloved trumpet. This was about the time that he began to have success in getting his drawings published. Gradually he worked his way into book illustration, and later into writing self-illustrated children's books. *Corduroy* was written in 1968, and at the time of Freeman's death in February 1978, a sequel, *A Pocket For Corduroy,* went to press. To attest to the popularity of his stories and illustrations, more than a million copies of his books are in print today.

From A POCKET FOR CORDUROY by Don Freeman. Copyright ©1978 by Don Freeman. Reprinted by permission of Penguin Putnam Books for Young Readers.

Corduroy
Published by The Viking Press

This song is just too good to resist, once you've read *Corduroy* to your students.

(sung to the tune of "This Old Man")

Corduroy was a bear.
He had no friends anywhere.
'Til a child named Lisa
Took him to her home.
Now that bear is not alone.

Michelle A. Therrien—PreK/K
Bright Horizons
Pittsfield, MA

If you have a stuffed bear that looks like Corduroy, you can generate lots of interest in the story even before you crack the book. Set your Corduroy look-alike in a reading corner along with a copy of *Corduroy.* If your bear has overalls, remove the button from one strap and leave the strap dangling. Once you've introduced him to students, encourage them to read to the bear. His favorite book is *Corduroy,* of course!

Jane Chastain—Gr. K, Holly Springs Elementary School, Pickens, SC

Preschoolers love to see the filmstrip of *Corduroy.* After showing it to your students, give them opportunities to retell the story in their own words. Show the filmstrip with no narration. As each filmstrip frame is shown on the screen, have a student explain the action. It's a great way to encourage vocabulary growth.

Beth Taylor—Pre/K, East Northport, NY

Make some Corduroy cupcakes after reading the book. Decorate cupcakes with chocolate icing. To give them a fuzzy, bearlike look, dip them in a bowl of cookie crumbs. Use tubed icing to add facial features. Then poke round chocolate cookie miniatures into the icing for bear ears.

Lynette Pyne, Plainsboro, NJ

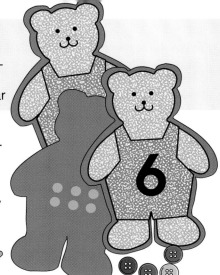

After reading *Corduroy* aloud, have your students make bears that resemble the furry guy in the story. To begin this project, use a bear-shaped sponge and brown paint to make a bear print. Sponge-paint an overall cutout (sized to fit the sponge-printed bear) using a small sponge square and paint. When the sponge-printed bear is dry, cut out the design, and glue the overall cutout to it. Use a marker to add a few facial details. Attract lots of attention by using these bears as a bulletin-board border or to line a hallway.

Lynette Pyne, Plainsboro, NJ

Each of your students can take home a stuffed bear, if you use this idea. Have each student cut out two identical bear shapes duplicated or drawn on heavy brown paper. Assist each student in gluing around the upper outline of one of his bear cutouts and pressing the other cutout onto it. Once the glue has dried, assist each student in stuffing cotton balls between the bear cutouts, before gluing the lower parts of the cutouts together. Give each student front and back overall cutouts to glue to his stuffed bear. Then encourage each student to decorate his bear as he desires using the available supplies. Now when a student wants to retell *Corduroy*, he'll have a bear to do it with.

Marianne Comstock
Frances Starms Early Childhood Center
Milwaukee, WI

Each weekend, send a Corduroy look-alike home with a different student. Explain that Corduroy travels in his own suitcase. Show students Corduroy, the suitcase, a copy of *Corduroy,* a letter of explanation for parents, and a page for dictating and drawing about Corduroy's adventures. Mention that older brothers and sisters, as well as parents, can assist the student with writing something about Corduroy's weekend, but that the student is to draw the picture himself. On Monday morning, when Corduroy comes back to school with his companion, the student explains his illustration to his classmates and adds it and the dictated story to a class book called "Corduroy's Weekend Adventures."

Gloria Bartoloni and Michelle Prentice-Smith—Gr. K
Mabel Paine Elementary
Yorba Linda, CA

Students can take great pride in making extra sponge-printed bears (like those described above) to be used in your learning centers. Label the front of each of ten bear cutouts with a different numeral from *one* to *ten*. Attach a corresponding number of sticky dots to the back of each cutout. Supply a basket of buttons or bear-shaped graham crackers to be used as counters. To use the center, have a student place the bears faceup, count out buttons or crackers to match each bear, and flip the bears to check his work.

Lynette Pyne

After reading *Corduroy,* have your students dictate new versions of this story for a classroom book. Remind students that Lisa bought Corduroy with money that she had saved. Ask students to brainstorm things that they would like to buy with money that they have saved. Then have each student dictate a new version of the story from his perspective and based on a purchase he would like to make. Write each child's response on a bear-shaped booklet page. Have the author illustrate his version before binding the pages into a booklet.

Lynette Pyne

To strengthen your students' color-identification skills, have them play this game. Place several buttons of various colors in a cloth pocket made for this game. Cut a card from construction paper to match each color of button in the pocket. Choose one child to play the role of Corduroy and ask him to leave the group for a moment. While Corduroy is away from the group, hold up a color card for the other students to see. Then lead them in singing the song which follows. Have Corduroy return to the circle, look through the pocket, and take out a button of the color mentioned in the song. Continue to play this game, having different students play the role of Corduroy and featuring a different color word each time the song is sung.

(sung to the tune of "Where Is Thumbkin?")

Corduroy, Corduroy,
We need you. We need you.
Please find a **blue** button.
Please find a **blue** button.
We thank you. We thank you.

Lynette Pyne, Plainsboro, NJ

For a unique sensory activity, ask parents to donate a variety of textured fabric scraps (such as seersucker, flannel, burlap, velvet, gingham, satin, or denim). Be sure that a scrap of corduroy is included in your fabric scraps. Cut the fabrics into simple overall shapes. Have the students touch each of the fabrics and describe the texture. Identify each type of fabric, if the students are unable to identify it themselves. Have each child choose an overall cutout to glue on a tagboard bear shape. Encourage each child to think of a name for his bear that is indicative of the texture of the bear's overalls. Students are likely to have bears named Silky, Fleece, Blue Jean, or Velvet.

If desired, convert these elements into a learning center. Label each of several bear cutouts with the name of a fabric and glue on a small swatch of the fabric. Using the same fabrics, cut pairs of overalls to match the swatches. Place the overalls in a bag and the bears on a table. Have students take turns feeling around in the bag for overalls to match each bear's swatch and "dressing" each bear.

Lynette Pyne

Mary Sutula—Preschool
Orlando, FL

A Pocket For Corduroy
Published by The Viking Press

After reading the story *A Pocket For Corduroy*, return to the part of the story when the artist was watching the dryer. Have the children take turns making spin art pictures that look like what the artist saw when he watched the dryer. To do this, cut art paper in a circle the size of a record album to go on a record player's turntable. Tape the paper to the turntable, before turning the record player on. As the paper rotates, have a student use paint and paintbrushes to decorate the paper. If desired, staple each student's dried artwork onto a dryer cutout designed to be similar to the dryer in *A Pocket For Corduroy*.

Cara Schlotter—Preschool
Faith Christian Child Care
Washington, IL

After reading *A Pocket For Corduroy*, have each student make a contribution to a class-made book. Duplicate a page bearing the incomplete sentence "I would like to find _____ tucked inside my pocket." Then have each student cut out and label a pocket shape. Assist each youngster in gluing the pocket to his copy of the duplicated page so that the top of the pocket remains open. On an index-card half, have each child draw something that he'd like to have in his pocket. Fill in each student's blank in the sentence with the word that he dictates, and show him how to tuck the card halfway into the pocket. Bind all the students' pages into a class book titled "A Pocketful Of Fun."

I would like to f
chocolate candi
tucked inside
my pocket.

Ben

Ginny Phelps—Language Development
Parkland Elementary
Rochester, NY

Norman The Doorman
Published by The Viking Press

After reading *Norman The Doorman*, set aside a day to be Norman Day. Have students help you prepare for the occasion by attaching circular mouse-ear cutouts to paper headbands so that each of them can be a mouse like Norman. Convert the classroom door into a mouse hole by taping poster board to the upper door frame, creating an arched entry. On Norman Day, have mouse-eared students take turns serving as the doorman throughout the day. Provide several colors of inexpensive bell wire, and encourage each student to use the wire to create an original wire sculpture masterpiece. Display these sculptures on a tabletop. And, by all means, in honor of Norman, visit a museum on Norman Day.

Rita Beiswenger—Preschool, Crescent Avenue Weekday School, Ft. Wayne, IN

Dandelion
Published by The Viking Press

Prior to reading *Dandelion*, ask each child to bring a photo of himself from home. Using a photocopier, make an enlarged copy of each photo. Read aloud *Dandelion* and discuss the changes the lion made in his appearance; then ask each child to use miscellaneous art supplies to change his enlarged photo. Encourage children to imaginatively color, paint, and glue things on to improve upon the original photo. When the transformed pictures are complete, have students match the original photos to the new, improved versions.

Mary Sutula—Preschool, Orlando, FL

After reading Don Freeman's *Dandelion*, have your own classroom tea party. Feast upon edible Dandelion cookies and "lion-ade." To make the eyes for the lion cookies, attach brown M&M's® or raisins to vanilla wafers with frosting. Similarly attach two pieces of candy corn for the lion's nose and mouth. Embellish the lion further by attaching string licorice whiskers and sprinkling orange- or yellow-tinted coconut around the wafer for the lion's mane.

"Lion-ade" is lemonade and orange juice mixed together and topped with floating lions. The floating lions are made by using orange and lemon slices, grape and strawberry halves, and raisins. Arrange these elements as shown and set these dandy lions afloat on the juice mixture before serving the "lion-ade."

Dawn Spurck
Creative Play Center
Colorado Springs, CO

A Rainbow Of My Own
Published by The Viking Press

Here's a taste-tempting follow-up for *A Rainbow Of My Own*. Make six large rectangular pans of flavored gelatin: one each of red, orange, yellow, green, blue, and purple. Cut the gelatin into small cubes. Put each color of cubes in a different bowl. Then have each student scoop some gelatin of each color in order into a clear plastic cup. Some youngsters may think their rainbows look too good to eat. Yum!

Mary Sutula—Preschool

After listening to you read aloud *A Rainbow Of My Own*, your little ones will be wanting a rainbow of their own, too. On a bulletin-board background, draw the arches to outline six color bands of a rainbow. Encourage the students to contribute red pieces of paper, cloth, and other materials to "colorize" the top band made by your arches. Provide glue and staplers for this purpose. On another day, have students attach orange pieces of paper, cloth, and materials to the next band on the board. Continue in this manner, having students glue yellow, green, blue, and purple items onto the bulletin board to complete the rainbow. When the work is finally done, your students will have a rainbow of their own.

Allison Pratt
Fauver Hill Kindergarten Center
Onalaska, WI

The Chalk Box Story
Published by HarperCollins Children's Books

The Chalk Box Story is a magical story about a box of talking chalk sticks who pool their talents and create a colorful story about a boy marooned on a desert island. To introduce this story, tack up a sheet of art paper where students can easily see it and place a box of colorful chalk sticks near the paper. Then tell the story from memory as you draw the associated illustrations on the paper. Afterward read the story aloud from the book, sharing Freeman's illustrations as you do. Then provide chalks and paper, and have each student make his own chalk-box story illustration. Have volunteers share their illustrations and the related stories with their classmates.

Chris Nelson—Gr. K, W. Coventry School, Coventry, RI

Little Thunder
Using Paul Goble's Books In The Classroom

Little Thunder makes a big impression when it comes to children's books about Native Americans. "Little Thunder" is the translation of the Native American name that was given to Paul Goble. As a young English lad, Goble developed an interest in and a respect for the Native Americans of the Great Plains. After spending several summers on Indian reservations and being adopted by Yakima and Sioux tribes, he moved to the United States.

One of the original reasons Goble retold Native American myths and legends was to increase the sense of pride that Native American children felt for their culture. Another of his purposes is to preserve bits of the culture for future generations. Each of his books emphasizes the harmonious relationship between man and nature, which has traditionally been an important aspect of Native American life. Building on children's natural curiosity and love of animals, Goble retells legends, hoping that the stories will help children be inspired by nature, as well as be respectful of it.

Paul Goble is quoted as saying, "To learn something of another culture has given me more facets and perspectives for my own life." Add some new facets and perspectives to the lives of your youngsters by introducing them to the Native American tales retold by Paul Goble —who's also known as Little Thunder.

Before beginning Native American studies, bring yourself up-to-date on current concerns regarding stereotypes and misinformation related to Native American cultures. Several educators expressed their concerns and discussed their methods in both the September 1992 and the January 1993 issues of Young Children, the journal of the National Association for the Education of Young Children. The comments are thought-provoking and informative, and reading them may be an excellent first step in preparing to discuss Native American cultures with your students.

The Gift Of The Sacred Dog

Published by Bradbury Press

In this Reading Rainbow Book, Paul Goble illuminates the story with colorful, glowing illustrations. He conveys the reverence and respect that Native Americans have for their Sacred Dog—the horse. When the Sacred Dogs were delivered from the sky to the Sioux, their beautiful colors were a lovely sight. Have your students work together to make a large, colorful horse for your classroom. Enlarge an outline of a horse onto bulletin-board paper using an opaque projector. Have students glue colorful tissue-paper strips within the outline to fill the shape. Cut out the horse design when dry and mount it on a bulletin board along with clouds made of cotton batting and a mane of tissue-paper strips.

The Girl Who Loved Wild Horses

Published by Bradbury Press

This Caldecott Medal winner is the story of a young Plains Indian girl and her love for horses. Beautiful illustrations set the perfect scene for this romantic story. Goble draws an illustration in pencil; then he traces it in India ink. Then he applies paint. When painting around a painted illustration, he doesn't always paint right up to the black line, but leaves a margin of white around what has previously been rendered. After looking for this in *The Girl Who Loved Wild Horses,* have your students create these art projects that also have white bands. First have each student use a large stencil to sponge-paint a horse (or other) shape. When the paint is dry, have each student trace his design with a black marker. Then have him paint the remainder of the page, leaving a margin of white around the horse.

The Great Race Of The Birds And Animals

Published by Bradbury Press

This Cheyenne and Sioux myth is a great way to start discussions about animals of the Great Plains—especially buffalo. After reading the story have students reexamine the illustrations in the book. Ask them to name the animals illustrated as you note each one on the board. Also ask them to provide a word telling how each animal might have moved (for example: Jack-rabbit hopped, Coyote trotted, and Turtle plodded). When your list is complete, have each youngster draw and cut out one animal to be used in a bulletin-board race scene similar to those in the book.

Dream Wolf

Published by Bradbury Press

Dream Wolf is a story of kinship between man and nature. After reading the book, ask students to retell the ending in their own words. Discuss the fact that, as more and more land is developed, people encroach more and more on what were natural lands. Find out how your students feel about this. Ask them to propose ways for man and nature to live in harmony.

Iktomi And The Boulder
A Plains Indian Story

Published by Orchard Books

In the folklore of the Plains Indians, Iktomi plays the role of the trickster. But his conceit gets him into trouble. Iktomi's thoughts are printed in small type and the narrator's comments are in italicized type. Audience participation is invited, making it even easier for children to enjoy the humor and the message. Ask students why they think Iktomi left his blanket on the boulder. Then have students recommend other ways that Iktomi could have dealt with the heat and ways that he could have avoided the problem altogether.

More Paul Goble Books

Star Boy
Buffalo Woman
Death Of The Iron Horse
Her Seven Brothers
I Sing For The Animals
Iktomi And The Buzzard: A Plains Indian Story
Iktomi And The Buffalo Skull: A Plains Indian Story
Iktomi And The Coyote: A Plains Indian Story

The Exceptional
Eloise Greenfield

Your students will be lured to explore relationships, emotions, and imagination with the prose and poetry of Eloise Greenfield. Before becoming an author, Eloise had always wanted to help improve the lives of her family, friends, and neighbors. Later she became inspired to write books for and about children—specifically African-American children. Eloise Greenfield worked diligently for many long hours to learn how to be a successful writer. And her hard work and dedication paid off—since the early 1970s, Eloise has been a major voice in children's literature that celebrates family life, human relationships, and the internal strength of individuals. Share some of Eloise Greenfield's literature with your youngsters; then invite them to share some of themselves with you.

by Mackie Rhodes

Honey, I Love
Illustrated by Jan Spivey Gilchrist
HarperCollins Publishers

From a child's playful, observant, and emotional perspective, this captivating poem expresses some of the things to love about life. After sharing this book, invite youngsters to create their own books to express some of the things *they* love. In advance draw a half heart pattern similar to the one shown and duplicate several copies on tagboard; then cut them out to make tracers. Demonstrate how to use a tracer by placing the straight edge on a fold and cutting out a double thickness of the pattern to make a heart shape. Then have each child trace and cut out two white hearts and one red heart from construction paper. To make booklet pages, instruct each child to align and glue one side of a folded white heart to the left side of the red heart. Repeat the process on the right side of the red heart. Then encourage each child to write about (dictate) and illustrate something he loves on each page. (Or have him glue on pictures cut out of magazines.) Then have each child write the title "Honey, I Love" on the front of his book. Invite each child to share his book with a classmate and his family members.

Africa Dream
Illustrated by Carole Byard
HarperCollins Children's Books

As a girl recounts her dream of long-ago Africa, she describes some of the life and culture of the African people. After reading the book aloud, return to the page on which the new-old friends sing a hello song. Encourage students to name some different words they use to greet people. Then ask any willing volunteers to lead the class in singing hello songs that they know.

Afterward explain that in Swahili—a language native to Africa—the word used for hello is *jambo*. Have youngsters greet one another with this African greeting. Then instruct youngsters to form a circle. Play "Jambo" from the recording *Jambo* by Ella Jenkins (available from Smithsonian Folkways Recordings, 1-800-410-9815). Encourage students to sing along as they greet their new-old friends in class with a song and smiles.

Night On Neighborhood Street
Illustrated by Jan Spivey Gilchrist
Dial Books For Young Readers

Youngsters will experience and relate to a range of emotions presented in this powerful collection of poetry depicting life and relationships. After sharing the book, revisit "Fambly Time." After discussing the poem, brainstorm a list of things that a family can do together. Write student responses on a sheet of chart paper. Then review the list, having a volunteer place a star sticker beside any activity that can also be done as a class. Discuss how your class also constitutes a type of family—a class family. Then inform children that they will have the opportunity to participate in "fambly" time every day for a predetermined period of time. Each day invite a different student to select an activity for the class to engage in during a designated family time. As new ideas and activities arise over time, include them on the list of student choices. And *all* the little ones can call it "Fambly Time!"

On My Horse
Illustrated by Jan Spivey Gilchrist
HarperCollins Publishers
(This book is out of print. Check your library.)

An imaginary romp through the wild satisfies a child's wish to ride a horse without supervision. Read this book with your students. Then ask each child to close her eyes and imagine that she is riding a horse as she *listens* to the story again. Afterward arrange a course to represent some of the terrain mentioned in the book. For instance, a safety cone might serve as a bush, a chair might serve as a tree, and two parallel ropes could serve as a stream. In turn, invite each child to pretend she is riding a horse through the wild. Encourage her to pretend the horse is walking, trotting, and galloping as she negotiates the course. At the end of each child's turn, ask her to tell the group something special about her imaginary ride—such as a place she rode past or an animal she spied while riding.

49

Grandpa's Face
Illustrated by Floyd Cooper
Philomel Books

Tamika loves everything about Grandpa—especially his sturdy brown face that always tells her she is loved. But one day Tamika witnesses a very different expression on Grandpa's face—one that scares her and causes her to wonder if Grandpa could ever love her anymore. After sharing this story, guide youngsters to discuss the looks they see on the faces of people they know. Ask them to tell how each expression makes them feel. Then pass out some hand mirrors, prompting each child to observe his reflection as he practices making facial expressions to represent different moods. Afterward call on the acting abilities of your students. First choose one child to stand in front of the group. Whisper an emotion to that child and have him act it out while the rest of the class tries to guess that specific emotion. Continue playing until each child has had a turn to perform.

She Come Bringing Me That Little Baby Girl
Illustrated by John Steptoe
HarperCollins Children's Books

What a sickening feeling it gives Kevin to see all the attention his new baby sister is receiving. After all, she was *supposed* to be a boy—that's what he asked for! But Kevin's opinion of his sister begins to change as he realizes the importance of his big-brother role. Follow up this story with a class discussion to discover which students have younger siblings and to determine how they feel about being older siblings. Ask those students to share some things they do *not* like about having younger brothers or sisters. Then encourage them to tell some of the *good* things that go along with having a younger sibling. Extend the discussion by playing the song "Why Did I Have To Have A Sister?" from *10 Carrot Diamond* by Charlotte Diamond (produced by Hug Bug Music Inc. and available from Educational Record Center, 1-800-438-1637). Ask students to listen for the advantage mentioned in the song of having a little sister. Conclude the discussion by inviting youngsters to brainstorm other advantages and positive aspects of having a younger sibling.

First Pink Light
Illustrated by Jan Spivey Gilchrist
Writers And Readers Publishing, Inc.

Tyree wants to stay up all night in his hideout and surprise his dad upon his homecoming. After negotiating with his mother, they work out a comfortable compromise. Then, at the first pink light in the sky, Dad finally does arrive—but to a surprise very different from Tyree's original plan. Read this story aloud; then have students discuss some special times when they wanted to stay up late or all night. Were they allowed to do so? Did they stay awake? Then invite youngsters to make a project illustrating a similar situation. For each child, duplicate the chair pattern (page 52) on construction paper. Have the child write/dictate to complete the story starter. Ask each child to color and cut out his chair, then glue it to a sheet of construction paper. Next invite each child to draw a picture of himself, then cut it out and glue it to his chair picture. If desired, have each child glue on fabric scraps to resemble a blanket and a pillow. Mount each picture on a board titled "First Pink Light."

I wanted to stay up...

because I was trying to see when my Grandpa got to my house.
Jovan

More Literature By Eloise Greenfield

William And The Good Old Days
Illustrated by Jan Spivey Gilchrist
HarperCollins Publishers

Grandmama's Joy
Illustrated by Carole Byard
Philomel Books

Under The Sunday Tree
Illustrated by Mr. Amos Ferguson
HarperCollins Publishers

Pattern
Use with *First Pink Light* on page 51.

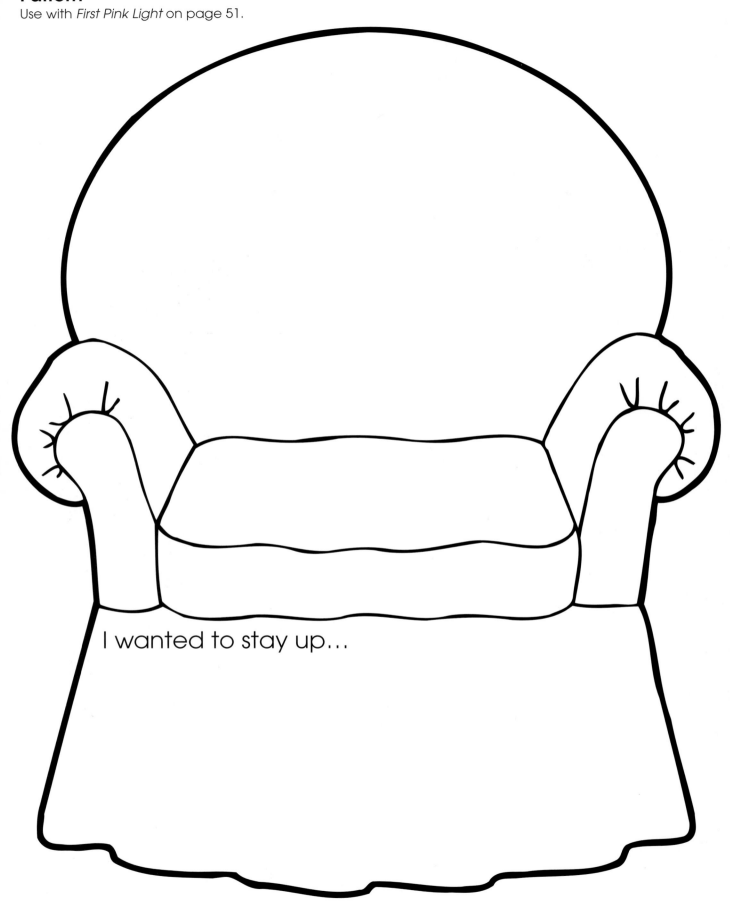

I wanted to stay up…

Kevin's Kids

Photo by Laura Dronzek

Your youngsters will just love getting to know the "kids" created by Kevin Henkes. Through the eyes and hearts of characters such as tender Chrysanthemum and imaginative Jessica, Kevin Henkes shares the trials and triumphs of childhood. He approaches his characters with understanding rooted in his own personal and family experiences. With humor and sensitivity, Kevin Henkes generates empathy and affection for all kinds of kids. And—being a kid-at-heart himself—he communicates lessons that will last a lifetime.

Chrysanthemum
Published by Greenwillow Books

Chrysanthemum loved her absolutely perfect name. She loved to hear it, to see it, and to write it. That is—until the first day of school. That's when Chrysanthemum begins to think that her name is absolutely dreadful! It is only through the gentle understanding of a perceptive teacher that Chrysanthemum is able to—once again—blossom!

With this activity your youngsters can discover and appreciate the uniqueness of their own names. First write each child's name on a separate slip of paper and place it in a basket. Then read the story aloud. Next write "Chrysanthemum" at the top of a piece of chart paper. Count together the number of letters in that name. Then ask each student to predict whether his own name is longer, shorter, or the same length as Chrysanthemum's. Next pick a name from the basket and write that name on the chart. After the children identify the name, count the letters in it. Encourage youngsters to compare that name to "Chrysanthemum." Periodically continue to pick names and add them to the list so that each child's name is written on the chart. Finally have each child write his name on a sheet of construction paper. Encourage him to embellish his name with his own personal style of art. Display each child's name above the appropriate letter on your classroom alphabet chart. What an absolutely perfect display!

Laura Titsch, Public School 171
Long Island City, NY

After examining their own names, encourage youngsters to brainstorm a list of flower names. Write their suggestions on chart paper. Then have each child write his name on a sticky note and place it beside the flower name he would like to have as his own. Extend this activity by having each student create his own unique flower. In advance, cut a supply of colored tissue paper into assorted shapes and sizes. Pour liquid starch into a shallow tray. Cut a sheet of waxed paper for each student. Using a paintbrush, have each child spread the starch onto his waxed paper. Then have him arrange tissue-paper pieces on the starch to resemble a flower. Encourage each child to give his flower a name. When they've dried, frame the flowers with construction-paper strips. Display these one-of-a-kind flowers on your classroom windows for your one-of-a-kind little ones to enjoy.

Nan Hokanson
Sheboygan Falls, WI

Rainbow Daisy

Bailey Goes Camping
Published by Greenwillow Books

Poor Bailey is too little to go camping—too little to join the fun that awaits his privileged older siblings. Then—to brooding Bailey's delight—Mama devises a plan that gives him the camping adventure of his life. After reading this story, have your very own class camping trip! Set up a small tent in the housekeeping area. Place nature items in the science center. Prepare a fishing game to put in another center. In the art area, provide materials to make a leaf-print project. During circle time, perform the rhyme and actions to "Going On A Bear Hunt," and tell silly ghost stories. And—for the finishing touch—have marshmallows for a snack!

Carmen Carpenter, Highland Preschool, Raleigh, NC

Owen
Published by Greenwillow Books

As the first day of school approaches, Owen is told that he cannot take his favorite blanket with him. But he just can't give up his not-so-fuzzy, yellow, go-everywhere, do-everything-with-him friend. After reading this story aloud, encourage youngsters to discuss how Owen feels about giving up his blanket. Find out if any of your students have had similar feelings. Then ask them to name some of their favorite things, and write their responses on chart paper. After discussing the items on the list, encourage each child to draw a picture of himself and his favorite thing. Have him write or dictate a statement about his picture. Display the pictures on a bulletin board titled "A Few Of Our Favorite Things."

Carmen Carpenter, Highland Preschool, Raleigh, NC

A Weekend With Wendell
Published by Greenwillow Books

This tale of a mischievous mouse and his antics during a sleepover weekend will be sure to spark talk and tales alike. After reading the story aloud, find out if your children have been on sleepovers. Encourage them to talk about their experiences. During the discussion, guide youngsters to suggest appropriate and inappropriate behavior for sleepovers. Then have your youngsters make sleepover pillows to serve as reminders for their next overnight stays. To start fold a sheet of 12" x 18" construction paper in half. Staple two sides together to resemble a pillowcase. Then assist each child in writing "When I sleep over, I will…," on her pillowcase. Next—on a sheet of 8 1/2" x 11" paper—encourage her to illustrate her completion to the sentence starter: this will be the pillow. When it's finished, slip the pillow into the pillowcase. Encourage each child to take her pillow home and place it in her suitcase. The next time she packs for a sleepover, she will find her pillow with useful reminders already packed.

Cathy Collier, Southeastern Elementary, Chesapeake, VA

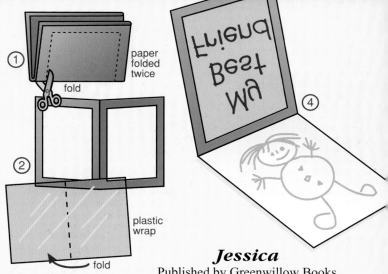

Jessica
Published by Greenwillow Books

Jessica, Ruthie's imaginary friend, goes everywhere and does everything with Ruthie. When Ruthie goes to kindergarten, Jessica goes right along with her. Then Ruthie discovers a new friend in a most surprising way. Prepare ahead of time to make these hide-and-seek pictures as a follow-up activity to this book. First make a class supply of picture frames. To make one, fold a sheet of 9" x 12" construction paper in half once, then again. Then—starting at the long folded edge—cut 3/4 inch from each side so that the middle section of the paper can be removed. Unfold the paper and it will look like a double frame. To make the "glass" for the frame, cut a 9-inch length of 11 3/4-inch wide, colored plastic wrap. Fold the plastic wrap in half. Placing the folded side of the plastic wrap along one edge of the frame, glue it in place over the opening. Then glue along the edges of the other side of the frame and fold it over the wrap. Trim away any excess plastic wrap. With a permanent marker, write "My Best Friend" on the plastic wrap. Place the frame aside until the story has been read. As you read the book, ask your children to look carefully for Jessica on each page. Engage them in a discussion about imaginary and real friends. Then give each student half of a 9" x 12" sheet of white construction paper. Using a crayon the same color as the plastic wrap in the frame, encourage each child to draw a picture of his best friend—real or imaginary. When each picture is completed, place a frame over it. Staple along the top edge. Your youngsters will have great fun lifting the frames to reveal their best friends.

More Books By Kevin Henkes
Published by Greenwillow Books

The Biggest Boy
(Illustrated by Nancy Tafuri)

Chester's Way

Grandpa & Bo

Julius, The Baby Of The World

Sheila Rae, The Brave

SHHHH

Perfectly Pat!

Pat Hutchins and Her Books

Pat Hutchins grew up in Yorkshire, England, where she started drawing at an early age. Her interest in drawing was apparently encouraged by an elderly couple, Mr. and Mrs. Bruce, who would give her a chocolate bar for each drawing that she did! But Pat thinks of herself as a writer first. She gets most of her story ideas by watching her own children, Morgan and Sam, or by remembering feelings or experiences she had in her own childhood. Today Pat works out of a tiny studio in her London home. Although she has been drawing for years, Pat still finds drawing very, very difficult. Each time she finishes a drawing, she is amazed that she has actually managed to complete the picture. Well, as we see it—they all turned out just perfectly, Pat!

Changes, Changes
Published by Aladdin Paperbacks

This delightful, wordless book will speak volumes to your youngsters! After sharing *Changes, Changes* with your class, divide children into small groups. Give each group a different set of building toys, such as wooden blocks, bristle blocks, and Legos®. Challenge each group to make something with their blocks. After five to ten minutes, take a picture of each group and its creation. Then explain that, just like in the book, each group is going to change its creation into something else. (Allow groups to switch blocks with another group, if desired.) After a while, take another picture of each group and its new creation. Repeat the process as long as there is student interest. Using the pictures from this activity, make a class book. Leave it wordless or have students dictate the text for each page. Either way, youngsters will have plenty to say about this book!

Sandie Bolze—Gr. K, Verne W. Critz School
East Patchogue, NY

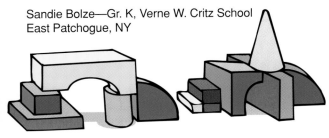

Strengthen the home-school connection by assembling a book-related traveling tote bag. Gather a supply of small blocks, your class book (from above), a notebook, and a copy of *Changes, Changes*. Place all of these items in a tote bag with a simple note of explanation to parents. Each day, send the tote bag home with a different child. Ask each child to share the books and blocks with his family. Have each child ask a family member to write about their shared experiences in the notebook provided. When the tote bag is brought back to school, allow the child to share his family's comments with the class.

Sandie Bolze—Gr. K

Titch
Published by Aladdin Paperbacks

Pat Hutchins's cheerful, cumulative tale, *Titch*, is an excellent choice for even the littlest of readers. After sharing this story, ask each child where he fits in his family. Is he the littlest? The biggest? In the middle? Then provide small groups of children with assortments of manipulatives, such as blocks, different lengths of straws or yarn, and commercial toy-building pieces. Ask each group to arrange its items according to size. Then encourage each group to discuss its arrangement by using vocabulary such as *little, medium, big* and/or *small, smaller,* and *smallest.*

Reading *Titch* can lead you and your class into discovering a scientific fact: *living things grow and change.* Explore this phenomenon by having each child plant her own sunflower seed and keep a journal to record its growth. For each child, prepare a journal containing several pages. Have her personalize and title the cover. Supply each child with a paper cup, a sunflower seed (available at seed stores), and some light potting soil. On the first page of her journal, have each child record/illustrate her supplies. Instruct her to almost fill the cup with soil, then gently press a sunflower seed into the soil so that the seed is covered with about 1/4 inch of soil. Have each child illustrate this stage in her journal. Then place the cup in a warm area of your room and keep the soil moist—not soaked. (Plant several extra seeds in case some of the children's seeds don't sprout.) Every few days—or whenever you notice a significant change—encourage youngsters to record the change in their journals. When the plants reach about six or seven inches and your climate is frost-free, plant the seedlings in the ground. Living things really do grow and change—just like *Titch!*

Donna Bishop—Gr. K
Stanley School
Swampscott, MA

Rosie's Walk
Published by Macmillan

Watch out—Rosie's in the barnyard, and the fox is close at hand! After sharing this book with your students, discuss the position words mentioned in the story. Then make "Hide The Hen" a daily event in your classroom for several days. When youngsters are out of your room, hide a toy hen or puppet somewhere in your classroom. At your signal, have youngsters try to find the hen. When a child has located the hen, have him announce, "I found the hen!" without moving it. Then, while everyone is watching, have him remove the hen from its hiding place; then ask children to use position words to describe where the hen was hiding. If desired, select groups of youngsters to illustrate each of the hen's hiding places. At the bottom of each illustrated page, write a dictated sentence to describe the hen's location. Combine the pages to make a class book that youngsters will enjoy again and again.

Lori J. Brown—Pre-K
Lebanon Valley Brethren Home Day Care Center
Palmyra, PA

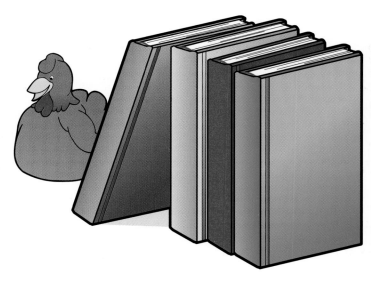

After following Rosie around the barnyard, youngsters will be primed to do some traveling of their own. Set up an obstacle course that requires youngsters to act out prepositions from *Rosie's Walk,* such as *across, around, over, through,* and *under.* Label each station with picture clues, or just call out the directions as youngsters arrive at each station in the course. After each child has learned the routine of the obstacle course, consider having each child choose to play a character of his choice and ad-lib another story with a chase scene similar to the one in *Rosie's Walk.*

Christy Owens—Gr. K
Centerville Kindergarten Village
Centerville, OH

The Wind Blew
Published by Aladdin Paperbacks

This blustery tale is a perfect prelude to "Wind-Powered Painting." After sharing the story, encourage your children to think about the power of the wind. Then explain that youngsters will be making wind-powered paintings. Cover an area of the floor with newspaper. Spread a length of butcher paper across the newspaper. Provide a basket of Ping-Pong® balls and other light balls, along with several colors of tempera paint. Begin by dipping one of the balls in a color of paint. Set that ball on the butcher paper. After reminding children that this is *wind-powered* painting, ask them to think of ways that the paper could be painted using wind. In moments, no doubt, children will be blowing and fanning up a storm! Continue in the same manner with additional paint-covered balls. (If desired, have each child make his own painting on an individual sheet of construction paper.)

Marsha Feffer—Pre-K
Bentley School, Salem Early Childhood Center

Children can experience the wonders of wind with these colorful, child-made wind socks. To make a wind sock, cut off the bottom of a paper lunch bag. Decorate the bag with glitter paint, neon construction-paper pieces, and stickers. Then attach crepe-paper streamers to one end of the bag. Attach a construction-paper handle to the opposite end of the bag. When the projects are completely dry, have children take their wind socks outside and experiment by running and dancing in the wind. What a blast!

Marsha Feffer—Pre-K

The Doorbell Rang
Published by Greenwillow Books

Pat Hutchins created a real crowd pleaser when she wrote *The Doorbell Rang.* After sharing the story with your children, prepare to act it out as a class play. Select children to play the roles of Ma, each of the children, and Grandma. Laminate and cut out 12 construction-paper cookies to use as props in the play. When your class is fully rehearsed and ready for the "real thing," invite parents or another class to see your play. Only *this* time, when Grandma walks in the door, give her a tray full of real cookies to share with the cast and audience members! Now that's a crowd pleaser!

Elinor Gesink—Gr. K, Sheldon Christian Kindergarten, Sheldon, IA

Extend the cookie theme from *The Doorbell Rang* to create this challenging center. Cut out and laminate 12 construction-paper cookies and 6 blank cards. Use a permanent marker to program each of the cards with one of the following numerals: 1, 2, 3, 4, 6, 12. Place the cookies and cards in a center, along with 12 small paper plates. To do this activity, a child draws a numeral card and places that many plates on a table. Then he divides all the cookies equally among the plates. Adapt this center for younger children by programming each cookie with a different numeral from 1–12. Place the cookies, paper plates, and a bowl of chocolate chips in the center. Have each child place each cookie on a different paper plate, then sequence them. Next have each child place the indicated amount of chocolate chips on each cookie. Provide a few unhandled chocolate chips for a special treat when the activity is completed.

Adapted from an idea by Carmen Carpenter—Pre-K
MacGregor Creative School
Cary, NC

A child-made recipe book can stimulate creative writing as well as provide a few chuckles for the adults with whom the recipes are shared. Have each child dictate a recipe for any type of cookie. Write his recipe on a sheet of construction paper; then have each child illustrate his recipe. Bind all of the pages between two construction-paper covers. Title the book; then have each child share his page with the class during a group reading time.

Adapted from an idea by Carmen Carpenter—Pre-K

More Pat Hutchins Books

1 Hunter (Published by Greenwillow Books)

Clocks And More Clocks (Published by Macmillan Books for Young Readers)

Don't Forget The Bacon! (Published by Greenwillow Books)

Good-Night, Owl! (Published by Aladdin Paperbacks)

Happy Birthday, Sam (Published by Mulberry Books)

Silly Billy! (Published by Greenwillow Books)

My Best Friend (Published by Greenwillow Books)

Tidy Titch (Published by Greenwillow Books)

The Surprise Party (Published by Macmillan Books for Young Readers)

The Very Worst Monster (Published by Greenwillow Books)

Three-Star Billy (Published by Greenwillow Books)

Where's The Baby? (Published by Greenwillow Books)

What Game Shall We Play? (Published by Mulberry Books)

Which Witch Is Which? (Published by Greenwillow Books)

You'll Soon Grow Into Them, Titch (Published by Greenwillow Books)

Keats In Class

Ezra Jack Keats, born March 11, 1916, showed an early inclination for the arts. He drew on everything in sight, with the approval of his indulgent mother. His father discouraged him from developing his talent, believing an artist could not make a decent living. Nevertheless, Keats continued to develop his talent, while his father watched on with silent pride. The lack of children's books available with young black heroes inspired Keats to create Peter, the black child who appears in *Whistle For Willie, Goggles, A Letter To Amy, Peter's Chair,* and *The Snowy Day* (winner of the 1963 Caldecott Medal). Keats believed, "If we all could really see each other exactly as the other is, this would be a different world. But first I think we have to begin to see each other."

Select from these ideas to introduce your youngsters to the unique styles and timeless appeal of Ezra Jack Keats's classics.

Amy's Letter

If your class is studying wind and air, *A Letter To Amy* (Puffin Books) can be an excellent literature choice. After reading the book, discuss with your youngsters the reasons why the letter blew away. For hands-on experiments with the force of wind, have students "write" letters. Then, keeping the children a safe distance from a fan, have youngsters take turns holding their letters in the air current and releasing them. Have youngsters compare the directions the letters took and the distances they traveled.

Marylee Sease—Gr. K, Meadowbrook Elementary, Canton, NC

A Show Of Creativity

A classroom pet show is a must following a reading of *Pet Show!* (Aladdin Paperbacks). Give your show a creative twist by asking that each child make a "pet" with the help of an adult. Encourage youngsters to make their pets with milk cartons, clothespins, egg cartons, buttons, fabric scraps, or any about-to-be-discarded item. Ask an adult to help the child name his pet and determine what kind of creature it is. On the day of the show, have each child show his pet and tell his classmates about it. Just as in the story, award ribbons to every show participant.

Debra Holbrook—Gr. K–4
Southern Baptist Educational Center
Southaven, MS

Snowy Science

Follow up a reading of *The Snowy Day* (Viking) by promoting some scientific observations. If it's snowy where you are, have a student volunteer make a snowball and place it in a jacket pocket. Hang up the jacket so everyone can see what happens as time passes. What can students determine from this observation? What happened to the snowball? Why did this happen? What is snow made of?

Nan Jungst
Willson Beardshear Early Childhood Center
Ames, IA

Footprints In The Snow

If your area is covered in new-fallen snow, it's a fine opportunity to read aloud *The Snowy Day* (Viking) and take a wintry walk. After making and examining tracks in the snow, bring youngsters inside to make some more-permanent tracks. Place a length of white bulletin board paper on the floor. At one end of the length, place a tub containing a mixture of light blue paint and liquid detergent. At the other end, place a towel and a tub containing warm water. Each student, in turn, steps barefoot into the paint, walks across the bulletin board paper, rinses his feet in the tub of water, and dries his feet. For added appeal, use a variety of pastel paint colors and sprinkle each damp footprint with clear glitter. When the paper is dry, post it on a bulletin board along with a drawing of Peter or another child.

adapted from an idea by Nan Jungst

adapted from an idea by Patsy Kirkland—Gr. K
Combee Elementary
Lakeland, FL

Who Needs The Real Thing?

What if you're a big fan of *The Snowy Day* (Viking), but there are no real snowflakes in sight? Here's the solution. Improvise with these snowball look-alikes. Have each youngster dampen Ivory soap flakes with water and form the mixture into a ball. Send each snowball look-alike home with a copy of "This Special Snowball."

Pennye Pucheu—Gr. K
Alice Boucher Kindergarten
Lafayette, LA

This Special Snowball
This special snowball is not to throw,
Because it's made of special snow.
By your sink it has a place,
To help you wash your hands and face.

A Sister In The House

Several of your students probably have young siblings at home. *Peter's Chair* (Puffin Books) is certain to touch some of the insecurities they've experienced as a result of having a little brother or sister around. After reading the story, ask students to name some of the things Peter found he had outgrown. Then find out what things your youngsters have outgrown themselves. Ask each child to get parental permission to bring to school something that he has outgrown. Suspend a sign over a display of these items that reads, "We're Much Bigger Now." For each child, write as he dictates at least one thing he can do now that he couldn't do when he was a baby. Have children illustrate these accomplishments.

That's A Hat?

Give your youngsters an opportunity to create collage artwork similar to that in *Jennie's Hat* (HarperTrophy). After reading the book aloud, draw a giant hat on a bulletin board. Beneath the hat, draw a face. Ask children to bring to school magazine pictures, wallpaper scraps, old buttons, bits of yarn, and bits of rickrack to decorate the hat. Have a student volunteer draw and cut out a picture of a bird's nest. Mount all of these elements atop the hat drawing. My, my! What a magnificent collage!

Michelle Keltner
Southern Baptist Educational Center
Olive Branch, MS

Shadows

Read aloud *Dreams* (Aladdin Paperbacks), and ask students if they ever have trouble falling asleep. Find out what shadows or shadowy patterns they've noticed as they were trying to drift off to sleep. Imagination often works overtime as people observe shadows. Put your youngsters' imaginations to work on shadowy shapes they can make at school. Give each youngster a sheet of construction paper. Have him drop a few spots of black or purple paint onto the paper. Fold each paper in half and press it with sweeping motions. Next have the student unfold the paper and imagine that the dark shape is a shadow. What could make a shadow shaped like that? Display these dried shadow paintings with student-dictated explanations of the shapes.

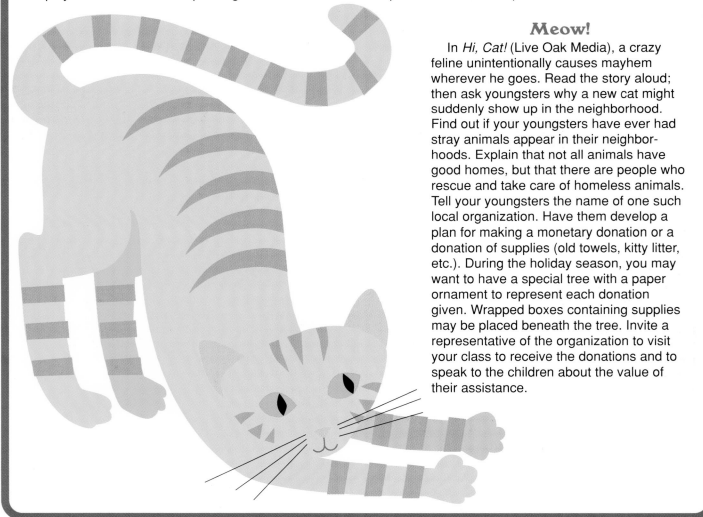

Meow!

In *Hi, Cat!* (Live Oak Media), a crazy feline unintentionally causes mayhem wherever he goes. Read the story aloud; then ask youngsters why a new cat might suddenly show up in the neighborhood. Find out if your youngsters have ever had stray animals appear in their neighborhoods. Explain that not all animals have good homes, but that there are people who rescue and take care of homeless animals. Tell your youngsters the name of one such local organization. Have them develop a plan for making a monetary donation or a donation of supplies (old towels, kitty litter, etc.). During the holiday season, you may want to have a special tree with a paper ornament to represent each donation given. Wrapped boxes containing supplies may be placed beneath the tree. Invite a representative of the organization to visit your class to receive the donations and to speak to the children about the value of their assistance.

Magical Goggles

If your youngsters study a letter a week, read aloud *Goggles* (Puffin Books) during "G" week for a great literature extension. Follow up by giving each student a pair of tagboard goggle cutouts with tinted plastic-wrap or acetate "lenses." Give each youngster a sheet of art paper on which a circle and a speech balloon have been drawn. Have each student decorate the circle to resemble his face, then glue the goggles in place. As each student dictates, write what he can see through his "magical" goggles.

Cathy McDougal, Palm Coast, FL

Goggle Making

It's easy to make goggles from six-pack holders and pipe cleaners. Collect plastic six-pack holders until you have one for every three children. Cut each holder into 3 two-hole segments. Demonstrate how to wrap pipe cleaners around each holder segment to create goggles. Provide assistance, if necessary, as each youngster makes his own goggles. Looks like it's time to read *Goggles!*

Lorna Vandersluis—Gr. K
Calvin Christian School
Grand Rapids, MI

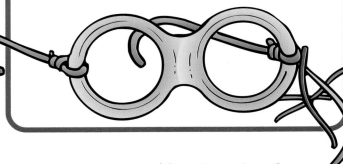

The Whistler And Willie

In *Whistle For Willie* (Viking), Peter thinks learning to whistle would be the greatest thing in the world! But despite several creative attempts, Peter just can't whistle. Then one day, a glorious sound comes from Peter's puckered lips. Peter can whistle! Have each student think of one thing he has recently learned to do. Find out how he feels about his accomplishment. Trace an oversize musical note onto several different colors of tagboard. Cut out (or have students cut out) at least one note for each youngster. As he dictates, write something about his accomplishment on his note. Suspend all of the completed musical notes in a cluster from the ceiling.

Who's In The Building?

Read aloud *Apartment 3* (Aladdin Paperbacks). Discuss the sounds the boys heard as they passed each apartment door. Have them re-create some of the sounds mentioned in the story. Then explain that we tune out lots of noises that could tell us what is going on around us. Have youngsters sit silently for a while, listening. Then discuss what they heard. Were they surprised by some of the things they heard? Repeat this exercise several times during the day at different locations in your building. It's amazing what you can hear when you really listen!

A World Of Goggles

After reading aloud *Goggles* (Puffin Books) explain that there are many different kinds of goggles. Have your students name a few different kinds, such as ski goggles, motorcycle goggles, swimmer's goggles, and safety goggles. Give each child a duplicated page bearing an oversize goggle outline that says, "Looking through my goggles I see…" Have each student decide on a type of goggles to "look through." Have him draw two pictures representative of what could be seen through that type of goggles. As he dictates, label each picture. Cut out each student's goggle outline. Then staple these cutouts between specially prepared goggle covers. Everyone's going to want to gaze through these goggles!

Lorna Vandersluis—Gr. K

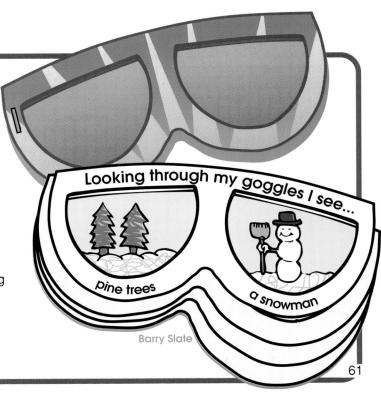

Barry Slate

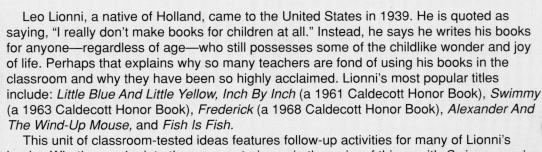

LIFE ACCORDING TO LIONNI

Leo Lionni, a native of Holland, came to the United States in 1939. He is quoted as saying, "I really don't make books for children at all." Instead, he says he writes his books for anyone—regardless of age—who still possesses some of the childlike wonder and joy of life. Perhaps that explains why so many teachers are fond of using his books in the classroom and why they have been so highly acclaimed. Lionni's most popular titles include: *Little Blue And Little Yellow, Inch By Inch* (a 1961 Caldecott Honor Book), *Swimmy* (a 1963 Caldecott Honor Book), *Frederick* (a 1968 Caldecott Honor Book), *Alexander And The Wind-Up Mouse,* and *Fish Is Fish.*

This unit of classroom-tested ideas features follow-up activities for many of Lionni's books. Whether you're into the mouse stories or in the swim of things with *Swimmy,* you're going to find lots of enticing ideas here and lots of meaningful learning in Leo Lionni books!

A Booklet Of Books

If you're going to be sharing several of Leo Lionni's books with your youngsters, have each child make a booklet with a page featuring each of the Lionni books read. Provide a tracer for the mouse-shaped booklet body that's nearly the size of a construction paper sheet and another tracer for the mouse ear. Trace the mouse-body shape onto two sheets of construction paper and several sheets of white paper. Trace the ear shape onto construction paper twice. Cut on each of the outlines. Cut a four-inch length of yarn for the mouse tail. Assemble the pieces into a booklet to resemble the one shown. Title and personalize the booklet. Each time a new Lionni book is introduced, have each child write the book's title on a booklet page and draw an illustration reminiscent of the book. When your Lionni unit is done, each student will have a neat booklet to take home.

Richelle Kreber and Sharon Roop—Gr. K
Slate Hill Elementary School
Worthington, OH

Tillie's Song

After reading aloud *Tillie And The Wall,* engage your youngsters in a lively chorus that recalls the story line.

Three Gray Mice
(sung to the tune of "Three Blind Mice")
Three gray mice, three gray mice,
See how they run. See how they run.
They all were chased by the farmer's cat.
They ran and hid in an old straw hat.
Did you ever see such a sight as that?
Three gray mice, three gray mice.

Linda Ferguson—Preschool
Elma Elementary
Elma, WA

A Tempting Treat

Follow up any of Leo Lionni's mouse books with this taste-tempting treat that youngsters can make for themselves. Have students prepare a batch of drop biscuit dough according to a recipe. Then demonstrate how to drop three dollops of dough onto a cookie sheet so that they will resemble a mouse head and ears when cooked. Have students place raisins on the dough for mouse eyes and noses. Bake the dough according to the recipe directions and allow each student to use a tube of icing to draw a smile onto her cooled biscuit. Yum! How about reading another Lionni mouse tale while everyone eats their biscuits?

Linda Ferguson—Preschool

On The Other Side Of The Wall

Tillie is a curious little mouse who wonders what is on the other side of a huge wall. Read aloud *Tillie And The Wall,* but stop when Tillie is digging under the wall. Have students brainstorm a list of things that Tillie will see on the other side of the wall when she breaks through. Have each student draw a picture of the world on the other side of the wall. Then finish the book. Find out if students like their endings or the one Leo Lionni chose better. Why? After a discussion, vote to determine which ending is preferred.

Jan Ross—Media Specialist
Dixie Elementary Magnet School
Lexington, KY

Wishing On A Purple Stone

In *Alexander And The Wind-Up Mouse,* a purple stone has magical powers. Read the story aloud. Then have students take turns holding a rock that has been painted purple. Have each student, in turn, tell what he would wish to be changed into. Note each student's answer on a different sheet of art paper. Then have students illustrate their wishes.

Mary Jo Sprunk—Gr. K
St. Charles School
Chippewa Falls, WI

What Will I Be?

Matthew's Dream is a wonderful story to use when studying community helpers, parents' careers, student aspirations, or any artist. After reading *Matthew's Dream* to the class, ask students what they might want to be when they are older. Together reexamine the illustrations in the book. Then provide bold colors of paint and art paper for youngsters to create their own original masterpieces.

Mary Jo Sprunk—Gr. K
St. Charles School
Chippewa Falls, WI

What A Darling Little Mouse!

Stimulate interest in Leo Lionni's mouse books by placing this mouse look-alike on a tabletop along with *Frederick, Tillie And The Wall, Alexander And The Wind-Up Mouse,* and other Lionni mouse books. To make a mouse, spray a plastic egg or L'eggs® container with gray paint. When the paint is dry, glue on felt ears, feet, and a tail. Complete the mouse with wiggle eyes. Hey, did you see this mouse? He looks a lot like Frederick!

Debbie Dodson—Preschool
Firestone Park YMCA
Akron, OH

Colorful Poetry

Follow up a reading of *Frederick* with a poetic activity. Begin by giving each student paints, a paintbrush, and a sheet of white art paper that has been cut into the shape of a visual imagery balloon similar to those in the book. Read aloud poems about color. (*Hailstones And Halibut Bones* is a good reference for these poems.) As you read, permit students to paint as the words inspire them. Have each student use art supplies to construct a mouse (see "Nice-And-Easy Mice") and tear newspaper into stone shapes. Mount the stone shapes on a bulletin board to make a wall. Then mount each youngster's painted visual-imagery balloon near his mouse on or around the wall.

Tracey Guest—Gr. K

Nice-And-Easy Mice

Frederick, Tillie, Alexander, or Matthew can be depicted with this construction-paper mouse made by each of your students. To make a mouse, cut a mouse-shaped body from construction paper. Add two circular construction-paper ears and a construction-paper tail and whiskers. Finish the mouse by drawing on eyes and a smile. Use these mice projects in conjunction with "Colorful Poetry."

Karen Waechter—Gr. K, Lowry Elementary
Tampa, FL

Mouse Ears

Follow up any of Lionni's mouse books by having each youngster make a pair of mouse ears. To make a pair of mouse ears, trace an inner ear–shaped cutout onto pink construction paper and an outer ear-shaped cutout onto gray construction paper. Cut out the ears, glue the parts together, and attach them to a tagboard strip cut to headband length. Once his headband is assembled, have each student dictate a completion for the sentence, "Frederick was special because…" Write his sentence on one mouse ear. Then have him dictate a completion for "I am special because…" Write this sentence on the other ear before stapling the headband to fit his head.

Tracey Gest—Gr. K, Houston Elementary, Austin, TX

Frederick was special because he was creative.

I am special because I am polite.

Wiggle Worm Walk

Introduce Leo Lionni's book *Inch By Inch* by having each youngster move like a worm before hearing the story. To begin, stand with your feet together, bend, and touch your hands to the floor just in front of your feet. Then walk your hands forward, without moving your feet, until you can't go any farther. Then walk your feet up to your hands. Continue repeating these steps to move around the room in a wormlike manner. Once everyone has the hang of the movement, play a compatible instrument recording to add to the fun of the exercise.

Linda Ferguson—Preschool
Elma Elementary
Elma, WA

Measuring Up

Read aloud *Inch By Inch.* Then give each youngster a laminated worm cutout. Encourage youngsters to measure classroom furniture and toys to determine how many worms long each item is. Then take youngsters outside and have them find out how many worms long the playground equipment is. To extend this type of activity into youngsters' homes, send notes of explanation home with the worms. It's a lively way to integrate language arts and the mathematical skill of measuring with nonstandard units.

Karen Galvin—Preschool
St. Clair Co-op Nursery
St. Clair, MI

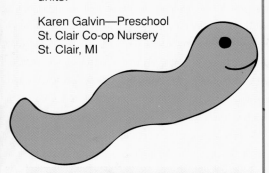

Inching Along

After reading *Inch By Inch* to your youngsters, have students use specially prepared inchworms to measure classroom objects. To make a worm, cut thick green craft yarn into one-inch lengths. Glue on two tiny wiggle eyes (or pom-poms) and dip the yarn ends in glue, if desired, to prevent fraying. When the glue has dried, present one of these inchworms to each student, and encourage him to measure books, shoes, scissors, and other classroom objects with the help of his worm. Then have each youngster express in complete sentences his observations about the lengths of the things that he measured. For example, "My pencil is about five inches long." What a fun-filled way to introduce standard measurement!

Cathy Conery—Gr. K
Martin Park School
Boulder, CO

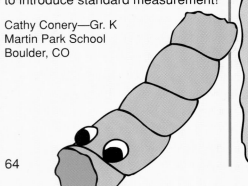

Wiggly Worms

Squeals of delight may be heard when you produce gummy worms as a follow-up activity for Lionni's book *Inch By Inch.* Pass each child a gummy worm from an assortment. Ask youngsters to closely observe their worms and name some of their characteristics (such as smooth, stretchy, red, green, etc.). Also have students compare their worms. Then ask each youngster to smell and taste his gummy worm, and brainstorm more descriptive words related to the smells and tastes of the treats.

Linda Ferguson—Preschool
Elma Elementary
Elma, WA

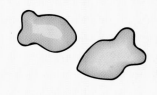

Swimmy Snack

Follow up a reading of Leo Lionni's *Swimmy* by having each youngster make his own ocean of fish to eat. Tint soft cream cheese blue by using food coloring. Spread the tinted cream cheese on a large rectangular cracker. Count out five or six fish-shaped crackers, and place them on the cream cheese. Take a moment to admire your ocean of fish before gobbling them down.

Linda Ferguson—Preschool

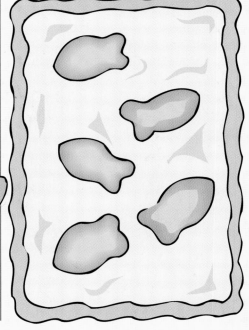

Fishy Bingo

After reading *Swimmy,* have each child draw (or trace) and cut out a large fish shape. At random, write six numerals between one and ten on each child's cutout. To play, call out numbers at random. Have each student cover the corresponding numerals with fish-shaped crackers. The first students to cover all of their numerals win the first round. Repeat the game as long as time permits. Allow youngsters to eat their fish crackers after you've played a few times.

Richelle Kreber and Sharon Roop—Gr. K
Slate Hill Elementary School
Worthington, OH

Color Exploration

Read aloud *Little Blue And Little Yellow.* Then make a color-mixing learning center available to your youngsters. Place cellophane circles of red, blue, and yellow on a white work surface in a center area. Encourage youngsters to experiment with the circles by overlapping them to create secondary colors. Youngsters may also want to reenact the story by using the circles.

Helen H. Warwick—Gr. K
First Methodist Day School
Marshall, TX

A Spin-off

After hearing *Little Blue And Little Yellow* and manipulating the color circles described in "Color Exploration," your youngsters may be interested in creating a class booklet patterned after Lionni's book. Choose another pair of primary colors to be the subject of your book (blue and red or red and yellow). Have each student illustrate a specific part of the story by gluing torn colored paper to a sheet of art paper. As he dictates, write about the illustration on the art paper. Staple the pages between tagboard covers bearing an appropriate title. Place this book in the classroom library for everyone to enjoy.

Linda Ferguson—Preschool
Elma Elementary
Elma, WA

Colorful Creations

After reading *A Color Of His Own,* enlist the help of each of your youngsters in making a shape booklet of chameleons. Ask each child to choose a color that he enjoys from a wide variety of colors. Then provide paint and have each youngster sponge paint a sheet of art paper with that color. When the papers are dry, have each youngster trace a large chameleon shape onto his page and cut the resulting outline. With a marker, have him add a facial expression to his chameleon. If desired, have each youngster dictate a sentence for you to write on his chameleon. Staple the pages into a booklet for everyone to enjoy.

Marian Beason—Developmental K
Seymour/Springview
Flushing, MI

Fishy Art

As a follow-up to *Fish Is Fish,* these colorful fish are great outlets for your youngsters' creativity. To make a fish, trace or draw a fish outline. Cut out this fish shape, trace it onto art paper, and cut out the resulting fish outline. Paint and decorate the two fish cutouts. (Be certain to paint the opposite sides of the cutouts so that when the fish is assembled, both painted sides will show.) After the paint has dried, staple the fish together with the painted sides out. Staple all but a few inches of the perimeter of the fish. Into the remaining opening, stuff tissue or discarded paper shreds. Staple the opening closed and attach a yarn hanger. Suspend each youngster's fish from your classroom ceiling for a sea of swimmers.

Richelle Kreber and Sharon Roop—Gr. K
Slate Hill Elementary School
Worthington, OH

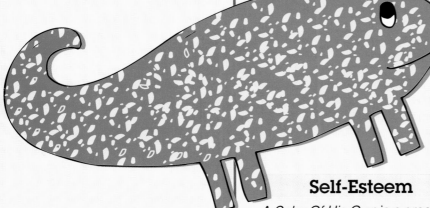

Sizing It Up

Several of Leo Lionni's stories teach the concept of size comparisons. *The Biggest House In the World* and *Swimmy* set the stage for learning about size differentiation! Before you know it, your children will be saying, "Enormous, gigantic, and immense," as well as, "Big, bigger, biggest!"

Pam Warren—Gr. K
DeSoto Trail School
Tallahassee, FL

Self-Esteem

A Color Of His Own is a great book to use to improve youngsters' self-esteem. After reading this book, have each child draw a self-portrait to emphasize his uniqueness. Also encourage each youngster to choose a color to be his own and to add that color to his drawings.

Laurie Henderson—Gr. K
Jordan Elementary
Beuna Park, CA

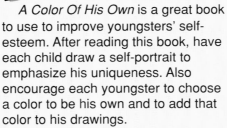

Classroom Publishing

"It's Ours!" is a fine classroom booklet to produce after a reading of Lionni's *It's Mine!* Provide youngsters with partially programmed pages saying, "We like…. It's ours!" After brainstorming several good completions, have each youngster write or copy a word or phrase to complete his page. Then ask each youngster to illustrate his sentence. Staple the pages between decorated tagboard covers bearing the title "It's Ours!"

Lorna Vander Sluis—Gr. K, Calvin Christian School, Wyoming, MI

Stamped Fish

Collect large Styrofoam® meat trays to make these eye-appealing fish prints after reading *Fish Is Fish.* To begin, cut the sides from a meat tray. Use a permanent marker to draw the outline of a fish that nearly reaches the edges of the tray. Then draw on additional details such as an eye, gills, and scales. Using a pencil with a dull blunt lead, trace over each of the lines on the tray. Then use the pencil to punch holes in the fish outline. Very gently press on the fish design until it detaches from the surrounding Styrofoam® surface. If desired, glue an empty thread spool to the back of the Styrofoam® printing surface. Paint the fish design with tempera paint; then press the design onto art paper, being certain to exert pressure evenly over the entire design. Rinse the fish design and repeat the process using another color of paint. Repeat this process as many times as desired.

Use this method to create fishy T-shirts by substituting fabric paint for tempera paint. It's an idea that will make a big splash with your youngsters!

Carol Aitken—Intern Teacher, Deer Park Elementary
New Port Richey, FL

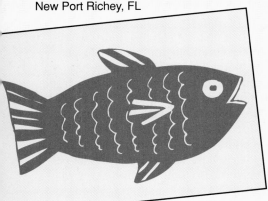

Appealing Aquariums

This unique aquarium is a wonderful keepsake to take home after reading the story *Fish Is Fish.* To make an aquarium, wash a clear plastic two-liter bottle. Fill the bottom of the bottle with aquarium rocks and shells. Fill the container with water or blue-tinted water. Remove the blue vinyl liner from a bottle cap and cut it into a fish shape. Attach a fishing weight to the end of a string. Glue the string to the belly of the fish cutout. When the glue is dry, drop the fish into the bottle. (Make additional fish from small pieces of vinyl, if desired, and prepare them as described previously.) Screw the cap tightly onto the bottle to complete the project. Hey, look at my fish!

Betty Kobes
Kanawha Elementary School
Belmond, IA

Wings Of Gold

Each of your youngsters can make a bird with golden wings like the one in *Tico And The Golden Wings.* (This book is out of print. Check your library.) Using the patterns on page 67, provide a brown construction-paper bird body pattern for each youngster and a tracer for the wings. While youngsters cut out the bird bodies, prepare gold foil for the wings by using a glue stick to glue two sheets of foil together with the right sides out. Then have each youngster trace the wing pattern onto the prepared gold foil paper and cut on the outline. Cut a slit where indicated in each child's bird cutout. Have each youngster insert his wing cutout into the slit and staple it near the slit. Youngsters can finish their birds by gluing a wiggle eye on each side of the cutout and attaching a yarn hanger.

Marian Beason
Seymour/Springview
Flushing, MI

Imagination

Have each of your youngsters contribute to an imaginative book inspired by a reading of Lionni's *Pezzettino.* (This book is out of print. Check your library.) Provide one-inch squares cut from lots of different colors of construction paper. Also provide glue and a sheet of art paper for each child. Have each student select, arrange, and glue squares to make a picture. Then compile the pages between decorated construction-paper covers, and add this booklet to your reading corner.

Marian Beason—Developmental K
Seymour/Springview
Flushing, MI

Letter Leaves

Read aloud Leo Lionni's *The Alphabet Tree.* Then get your youngsters busy making leaf prints or rubbings. Have each student cut out a print or a rubbing and write a letter of the alphabet or a sight word onto the leaf. Have each youngster attach her leaf to a paper tree branch mounted on a bulletin board. This attractive display will be a great reminder of the letters or words that youngsters have learned.

Richelle Kreber and Sharon Roop—Gr. K
Slate Hill Elementary
Worthington, OH

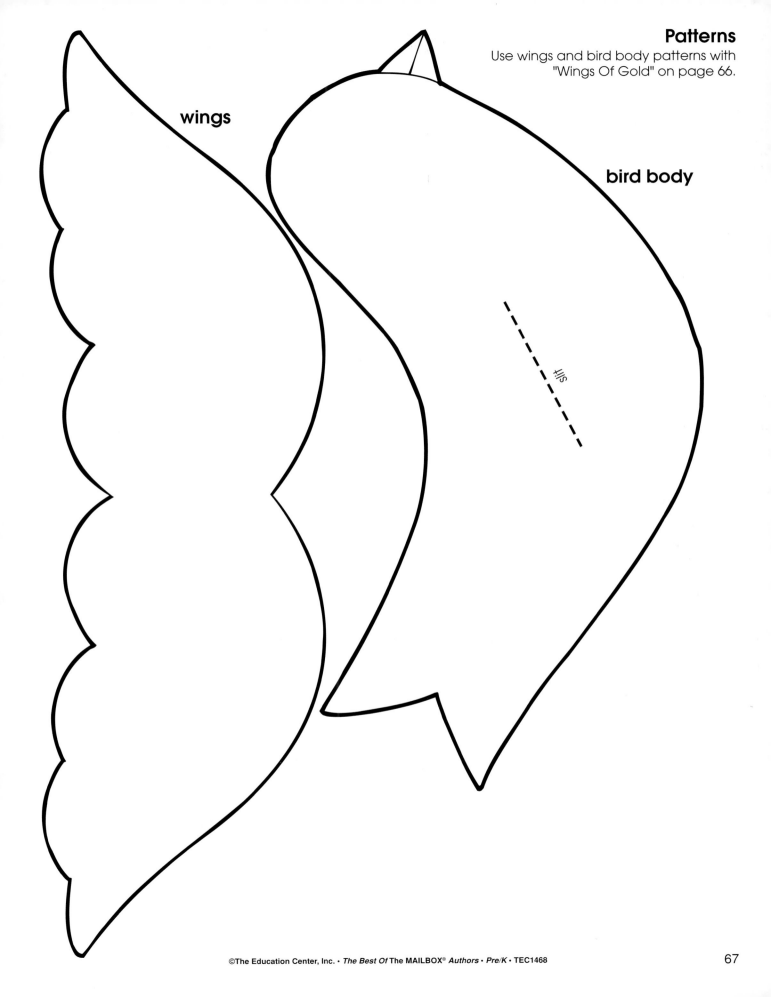

Patterns

Use wings and bird body patterns with "Wings Of Gold" on page 66.

wings

bird body

slit

Bill Martin, Jr.
Sharing The Joy And Importance Of Reading

Illustration from *Brown Bear, Brown Bear, What Do You See?* copyright © 1992 by Eric Carle. By permission of Henry Holt & Company.

In 1945 Bill Martin, Jr., wrote his first book, The Little Squeegy Bug, *that was illustrated by his brother Bernard. When Martin visited bookstores and drugstores with the book, it began to sell, but after First Lady Eleanor Roosevelt mentioned his book on the radio, sales soared to more than half a million.*

As Martin worked on other books with his brother, his interest in children's reading and education grew. So he went back to college and became an elementary school principal. His work in education convinced him of the importance of stimulating early reading experiences. In 1960 Martin became an editor and writer at Holt, Rinehart & Winston. A few years later he contacted a freelance artist to illustrate a book he'd written. That book, Brown Bear, Brown Bear, What Do You See?, *not only became one of the best-loved picture books of all time but also launched the illustrating and writing career of the artist who brought it to life—Eric Carle. In the 1980s Martin met and enlisted the coauthorship of John Archambault, with whom he had collaborated on several books and shares a common interest in helping children discover the joy of reading. Martin continues to be a freelance writer and editor, and he tours the United States speaking to teachers about reading, literacy, and the whole-language approach.*

"Martin-ize" your classroom with these books written or cowritten by Bill Martin, Jr. Then get your students personally involved with each story by using the suggestions provided.

An Old Favorite

Follow up a reading of *Brown Bear, Brown Bear, What Do You See?* by inviting youngsters to cut brightly colored finger-painted paper into the shapes of animals. Have one child create a brown bear or make one yourself. Have each youngster embellish his animal cutout and glue it to a sheet of art paper. Stack the papers so that the bear is on top, and staple them between tagboard covers. Then have students dictate dialogue similar to that in the book as you record it on each booklet page. Gee, Brown Bear, there's a world of things to see!

A New Arrival

Who's new in the zoo? Polar Bear, that's who, and he's hearing all kinds of noises. He's making all kinds of noises as well as he claws his way up in popularity by appearing in *School Library Journal's* "Best Books 1991" list and selling more than 172,000 copies in his first year. Read aloud *Polar Bear, Polar Bear, What Do You Hear?* written by Bill Martin, Jr., and illustrated by Eric Carle. Then have each youngster choose an animal. Provide supplies so that each youngster can decorate a paper plate mask to resemble the animal he selected. When the masks are done, read the story aloud or have a youngster read it. As his animal is mentioned, have each child parade in front of the class wearing his mask and making the appropriate ruckus.

Up The Coconut Tree

Chicka Chicka Boom Boom is one of several titles that Bill Martin, Jr., coauthored with John Archambault. Its perky illustrations are the work of Lois Ehlert. It's an instant hit in a preschool or kindergarten class due to its rhythm, rhyme, alphabet characters, and predictable plot. Read this book aloud using a pronounced rhythm. Then enlist the help of a couple of student volunteers. Have one child hold maracas in two hands, and give the other child a drum. Instruct the maraca player to shake each maraca separately for one beat, and instruct the drummer to strike the drum for two beats. When this is done in repeated succession, it will sound like "chicka chicka boom boom." As your musicians play, read the story again keeping time with the beat. If your youngsters get a big kick out of this presentation, outfit the entire group for one large rhythm band to play background rhythms for the story.

Merry-go-round

Take a carousel ride without leaving the room. Bill Martin, Jr., and John Archambault teamed up to write *Up And Down On The Merry-Go-Round* (illustrated by Ted Rand), and it's a ride that your youngsters will beg for time and again. After reading the book aloud, play a recording of calliope music similar to that of a carousel ride. (Check any circus recordings in your library for something suitable.) As the music plays, have youngsters canter around in a circle as though they are merry-go-round horses. Later ask them to describe favorite carousel rides.

Bull Riders

White Dynamite And Curly Kidd (coauthored by John Archambault and illustrated by Ted Rand) is one rollicking rodeo of a ride! And just when you think you've got it all under your hat, you're in for a delightful surprise. Read the book aloud; then find out how many of your youngsters were surprised to learn that the bull rider's child was a girl. Find out whether they feel some jobs are better suited to one sex than the other.

Fetching The Milk

The Ghost-Eye Tree (coauthored by John Archambault and illustrated by Ted Rand) is a perfect selection for October. It takes place on a dark and windy night when a boy and his sister must pass a gnarly haunted tree on their way to get milk for their mother. Read the story aloud; then find out about your youngsters' after-dark fears.

Do-si-do

Barn Dance! (coauthored by John Archambault and illustrated by Ted Rand) is another tale that's just too much fun to pass by. Make the reading of this book a special event by dressing as a scarecrow and sitting on a hay bale. Have a square-dance instrumental recorder by your side, but do not turn the player on until you've read, "The scarecrow tucked the fiddle underneath his chin/An' fiddled out a welcome to all his country kin." Continue reading while the music plays until you read, "'Till they got so dizzy that they all fell down." Encourage students to stamp and clap until the music ends; then finish the story. Yee-haa!

Others Too Good To Miss

Be sure to ask your librarian for these books also by Bill Martin, Jr., and John Archambault: *The Magic Pumpkin, Here Are My Hands, Listen To The Rain,* and *Knots On A Counting Rope.*

If your library is missing any of the titles mentioned in this Bill Martin, Jr., unit, they may be purchased by calling Cornerstone: America's Source For Children's Literature at 1-800-58-BOOKS.

Mercer Mayer And His Marvelous Critters

Scores of children have enjoyed Mercer Mayer's handiwork in dozens of books. Mayer does not see himself as the creator of his characters and story lines; rather he believes they are "given" to him. He was quoted as saying, "One day I will sit down and wonder, 'will I ever think of another frog book?' 'Oh, probably not,' comes the answer, and then a few days later, there it is. One, two, three, I have the theme and the plot." Mayer insists he can't just "think up" a book. "I've now come to the conclusion that I am Frog's creation, which is just fine with me." He says his "main desire in writing and illustrating is to expand the childhood fantasy world which adults forget all about…." Share the fear, the courage, and the love. Share a Mayer fantasy.

Mercer Mayer doesn't really "do" monsters. He prefers to think of them as critters. The rest of us—the young and the young-at-heart—just like to think of them…, and read about them…, and imagine them. Browse through this selection containing the best of your colleagues' suggestions for using Mercer Mayer books in your early childhood classroom.

A Boy, A Dog, And A Frog

A Frog Of My Own

A Boy, A Dog, And A Frog was Mercer Mayer's first book. This wordless delight has a way of making most of us wish we had frogs of our own. Gather these paper components in preparation for making a frog: a 2" x 3" pink rectangle, two 3-inch-diameter white circles, and two 2-inch-diameter black circles. From green construction paper cut a 12" x 6" rectangle, a 9" circle, four 12" x 1" pieces, and four 3" squares.

To make a frog, fold the large green rectangle to a 6" square. For the frog's head and mouth, trim to round the corners opposite the fold. Bend and crease the rounded ends separately so that they are perpendicular with the folded paper. At one end of the pink rectangle, trim to round the corners for a tongue. Glue the untrimmed corners inside the mouth. Assemble and glue the eyes as shown. Attach the head to the green circle body. Then accordion-fold the strips for the frog's limbs. Attach them to the back of the circle. Trim the squares to resemble frog feet, and attach them to the dangling ends of the accordion-folded strips. At last, a frog of my own!

Katy Galewski—Gr. K, Sacred Heart School, St. Francis, WI

Frog Goes To Dinner

Good Enough To Eat

Mercer Mayer's popular series of books about Frog includes *Frog Goes to Dinner.* After reading this story aloud to your youngsters, have each of them make a paper salad for Frog. To make a salad, crumple green, tissue-paper lettuce and glue it to a small paper plate. Glue on a three-inch, red construction-paper circle for a tomato slice and several smaller, light green construction-paper circles for cucumber slices. Glue on paper replicas of other salad ingredients as desired. Give each youngster a frog cutout to pose and glue amid the salad ingredients.

Donna Hammond—Gr. K
Newport Elementary School
Newport, ME

There's An Alligator Under My Bed

And Then...

Videotape yourself or someone else reading aloud *There's An Alligator Under My Bed.* Pair youngsters for this exercise in creative thinking. Ask a pair to decide what must have happened after Dad read the note in *There's An Alligator Under My Bed.* Videotape the pair as they explain and/or dramatize how Dad finally got the alligator out of the garage. Then pause long enough for another pair to come up with the next segment of the story. Videotape them as they relate it to their classmates. Continue in this manner, videotaping every segment of the unfolding story. Suggest that the last pair might have the alligator end up at the zoo. You may be surprised how creative your youngsters can be in moving the alligator from place to place. Play the entire tape and enjoy the giggles.

adapted from an idea by Becky Gibson, Auburn, AL

See What's There Now

After reading *There's An Alligator Under My Bed,* brainstorm with your students to create a class story: *There's A(n) [animal of their choice] Under My Bed.* What if the alligator were gone, but in his place was another bothersome animal? As children dictate the plot, encourage them to solve the problems created by this creature. Copy the sentences into a big, blank booklet, and have students illustrate each page.

A variation of this suggestion is to have students work in groups of five. Each group is to propose a substitute animal to take the place of the alligator. Then each group member assists in dictating a new version of the story and in illustrating the resulting book.

Melissa Mosby—Gr. K, Roosevelt Elementary School, Tulsa, OK

Kathleen McCarthy—Gr. K, Frankfurt American Elementary School, Frankfurt, Germany

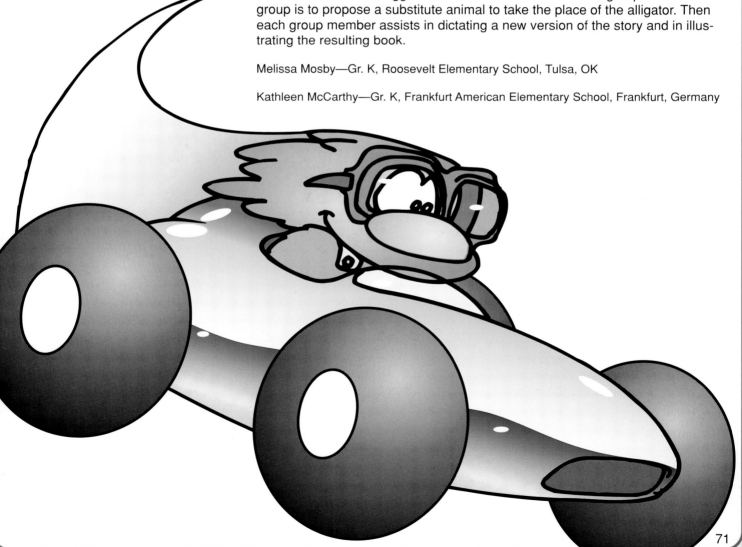

Beware!

Have your students take a close look at the illustrations in *There's An Alligator Under My Bed.* Call their attention to the warning sign. Challenge the students to find other books containing environmental print. Also ask them to take a closer look at the environmental print that they pass each day. Based on their observations, have them create some signs for your classroom.

Michelle Sears—Substitute Teacher
Glens Falls, NY

Read This!

The warning sign in *There's An Alligator Under My Bed* may give your youngsters the urge to make simple signs of their own. Give each youngster a sheet of paper and a marker or colored pencil. Reminding them that they can even write in code (scribbles) if they want to, have each of your youngsters create an original sign and tape it to your classroom door. This is a wonderful way to show emerging writers that there are different ways to write and that everyone can do it successfully!

Linda Bringman—Pre/K
Holland Elementary School
Holland, OH

Alligator Positioning

Youngsters are primed for position word practice after you read *There's An Alligator Under My Bed.* Have each youngster draw (or trace), color, and cut out an alligator. Then give each of them a bed cutout. As you direct, have each youngster position his alligator *above, below, on top of, beneath, to the right of, to the left of, over,* and *under* the bed. After each direction, scan the class to see who needs help. Finally ask each child to place his alligator wherever he'd like. Then, as you pass by him, have the child give a complete sentence telling the location of his alligator. When these cutouts go home, parents are likely to hear all about *There's An Alligator Under My Bed.*

Suzanne Grade—Gr. K
Dewey International Studies Magnet
   School
St. Louis County, MO

Alligators To Go

Changing a clothespin into an alligator is a task your youngsters will really enjoy sinking their teeth into. To make an alligator, paint a spring-type clothespin green and allow it to dry. Glue two small wiggle eyes near the closed end of the clothespin. This alligator looks great when clipped to a copy of the book!

May Alcoke—Gr. K
Oak Grove Elementary
Roanoke, VA

It Takes Coordination

In order to get to his bed safely, the little guy in *There's An Alligator Under My Bed* walked a plank. Your children can have a lot of fun dramatizing this part of the story. Set up a balance beam—or better yet—set up two, leaving a small gap between them. (If balance beams aren't available, put masking tape on the floor for your youngsters to walk on.) Place a toy stuffed alligator near the beam or the space between beams. Youngsters can try walking to the beam to the safety of an imaginary bed without falling off into alligator-infested territory.

Michelle Sears—Substitute Teacher

I Just Forgot

Remembering The Rules

For a little person, there are a lot of things to remember in a school setting. Read aloud *I Just Forgot,* and have your youngsters recall times when they have forgotten school rules. As a class, brainstorm the most important classroom rules. List each rule on a separate sheet of construction paper, and have students draw and color pictures or glue magazine cutouts to the pages to illustrate the rules. Keep this book in your classroom library. If someone forgets the rules, he can get a quick refresher course by looking through this student-made book.

Sarah A. Simpson—Gr. K
Pinar Elementary School, Orlando, FL

There's Something In My Attic

Come Down From There!

Before reading *There's Something In My Attic* to your little ones, use a paper clip to attach a piece of paper so that it covers each nightmare pictured. Once you've read the book aloud, ask each youngster to draw a picture of what he thinks the nightmare looked like. Have everyone show his picture to his classmates if he'd like. Reread the book, uncovering each picture of the nightmare as you get to it. No doubt, your students will be delighted with the uncovered critters.

Becky Gibson, Auburn, AL

There's A Nightmare In My Closet

They're Here

Read aloud *There's A Nightmare In My Closet.* Then provide scraps of colored construction paper and glue, and encourage youngsters to create one-of-a-kind "nightmares." Decorate a bulletin-board-paper length to resemble a closet door. Write the book's title and author on it. Mount this door on a bulletin board or empty wall space. Attach students' nightmares so that they appear to be peeking around the door. Peekaboo!

Karen Waechter—Gr. K, Bay Crest Elementary, Tampa, FL

Here's What Happened Next

After reading aloud *There's A Nightmare In My Closet,* have the students examine and discuss the last double-page illustration that shows a second nightmare coming out of the closet. Then ask for personal theories about what might happen next. Have each student draw a picture representing his theory. When everyone is finished, have youngsters share their pictures and thoughts with their classmates. You may be surprised to find a lot of diversity in their theories, but they'll be pleased that all answers are accepted.

Jan Ross—Media Specialist, Dixie Elementary Magnet School, Lexington, KY

Nightmare, Be Gone!

Just a light misting from this mysterious spray bottle and nightmares may indefinitely refuse to make an appearance. Clean an empty spray bottle; then fill it with water that has had a little mint extract and a few drops of food coloring added. Cover the sides of the bottle with Con-Tact® paper; then use a permanent marker to write "Nightmare-Be-Gone Spray" on the bottle. After reading *There's A Nightmare In My Closet,* spray your closets to rid them of any nightmares that might be lurking there.

Annaliese Turner—Pre/K, Hillsborough, NC

Nightmare Flip Book

This student-made booklet is perfect for prompting visual perception practice. For this flip book's backing, enlarge a nightmare outline onto poster board. Make an identical tagboard outline for each student. Have each youngster use a blue or black permanent marker to draw facial features, scales, stripes, polka dots, or any other design on his outline. The following day, have youngsters sponge paint their nightmares with their choice of several colors of thinned, bright tempera paint. Once dry, cut each tagboard nightmare into three equal horizontal sections. Punch two holes near the left edge of each section, lining the holes up on all identical pieces. Near the left edge of the poster-board book backing, punch six holes to match those on the sections. Use metal rings to bind each set of sections in place. Youngsters will love looking through this book to mix and match nightmares.

Claudia Marie Raab—Pre/K and K
Utah Schools For The Deaf And
   The Blind
Ogden, UT

When I Get Bigger And I Was So Mad

Growing Up

It's fun to be an author when you get to speculate about what your future holds. Read aloud *When I Get Bigger.* Then have each youngster dictate what he can't wait to do when he's bigger. Write his comments near the bottom of a sheet of paper. Then have him illustrate his comments. Collect the papers from all of your youngsters and bind the pages for a class-authored book titled *When We Get Bigger.*

Have youngsters similarly author another booklet after hearing Mercer Mayer's *I Was So Mad.* It's a great way to slip into discussions about feelings.

Lorna Vander Sluis—Gr. K
Calvin Christian, Wyoming, MI

73

Ah-Choo

Pass The Handkerchiefs

Mercer Mayer got the idea for this book as he was conducting a work-shop for elementary school teachers. In answer to a question from the audience, he was explaining how he creates a new book. He began to explain and draw. As he did, this story began to emerge. On his flight home, he fleshed out the idea on airline stationery.

Share *Ah-Choo,* a nearly wordless book, with your youngsters and then assist them in making a related art project. Have each youngster draw his facial features on a paper plate. Have him add hair and other details as desired. Then trace each child's lower arm and hand, and have him cut it out. Glue the arm end of the cutout to the back of the paper plate. Glue a tissue in what would be the palm of the hand. Bend the arm cutout so that the hand covers the mouth on the plate.

Another variation of this idea is to have each child draw a self-portrait on construction paper and cut it out. Paint his hand with tempera and have the child press it onto white construction paper. Cut out the handprint. Glue a tissue to the back of it; then glue the tissue to the mouth portion of the self-portrait. When these projects go home, parents are sure to hear about *Ah-Choo.*

Pat Marr—Gr. K, Taft School, Ferndale, MI

Dawn Hurley, Bethel Park, PA

What Do You Do With A Kangaroo?

Splish-Splash

Here's a lively project each of your youngsters will want to splash around in. To make this project, tape together a full-page, construction-paper bath-tub pattern (like the one shown) and a construction-paper pattern of a towel bar and towel. Then, from a towel pattern page (similar to the one shown), cut out and stack three tow-els. Staple the stack of towel cutouts atop the towel/towel bar design to create a booklet. Then glue three animal cutouts to Popsicle sticks to make stick puppets, and slit a hori-zontal opening in the bathtub. Com-plete one towel sentence for each stick puppet. Read the writing on each towel as you insert the matching stick puppet so that the animal seems to be taking a bath.

Kathy Curnow—Gr. K
Frank Constanzer—Art Teacher
Woolridge Elementary
Midlothian, VA

The New Baby

There's A Baby In The House

If any of your little ones have younger siblings at home, this book is really going to strike a chord with them. After reading *The New Baby* aloud, find out who has a baby at home, and have these youngsters compare notes on what new babies are like. Then find out what your entire group of youngsters likes best and worst about babies. Set up a dramatic play area including a changing table, diapers, baby dolls, baby clothes, bottles, rattles, small blan-kets, and other baby-care items. Encourage youngsters to play the roles of different family members and caretakers as they act out what it's like to have a baby around.

Marcy Becker—Preschool
Temple Beth Hillel Nursery And Kindergarten
Villanova, PA

McPhail's Menagerie

Do you have enough childlike wonder left that you can imagine helping an ailing potbellied bear rummage through the refrigerator in the middle of the night? Or can you empathize with a lion who makes a marvelously incredible discovery only to have it evaporate into thin air before he can share it with his friends? Or can you relate to Andrews's parents as they become increasingly exasperated by their son's bathtime escapades? If so, get ready for a menagerie of books crafted by David McPhail. Although he never took his childhood artwork seriously, as an adult he has made a serious—but comical—contribution to the field of children's literature in his dual role as writer and illustrator.

Pick your favorite McPhail books and use them with the accompanying activities. You're going to find each book to be a lively adventure, befitting this author/illustrator who believes that each day is a new adventure.

Andrew's Bath

(This book is out of print. Check your library.)

When Andrew told his parents about the animals in his tub, they paid little attention. But if your youngsters fill a bathtub with animals, lots of people will notice. Mount a giant bathtub cutout on a bulletin board. Then have each student paint a paper plate and glue construction-paper cutouts to it to create the head and neck of the large animal of his choice. Mount these creations so that the animals appear to be in the tub. Few people will be able to pass by this tub full of critters without pausing to take it all in.

Fix-It

This delightful tale points out the virtues of pulling the plug—the TV plug, that is. Have each child trim to round both corners at one end of a sheet of construction paper. To the back of the opposite end of the page, glue two narrow construction-paper strips for prongs. As the student dictates, write a great alternative to watching TV on the construction-paper plug. For the cord, attach a length of crepe-paper streamer opposite the prongs. Display these plugs on a bulletin board with the title "Pull The Plug On TV."

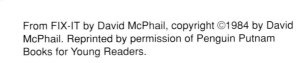

From FIX-IT by David McPhail, copyright ©1984 by David McPhail. Reprinted by permission of Penguin Putnam Books for Young Readers.

The Train

In his dream Matthew repaired the train and helped the stationmaster, the conductor, the engineer, and the fireman. Project the patterns for an engine, passenger car, and caboose (pages 33, 34, and 35) onto appliance boxes. Cut out the window areas and other openings. Then have children help you paint the train. Provide props related to the passengers and the workers on the train. Not only will you find that this is a great way to promote dramatic play, but the train also makes a lovely room divider.

Emma's Vacation

Sometimes the best part of a vacation is the part that's spent with loved ones and Mother Nature. Emma suggested wading in the brook, fishing, picking berries, climbing trees, picnicking, hiking, and resting in a hammock. Ask each youngster to draw a picture of a simple, nature-related activity that he most enjoys or believes he would enjoy. Post each picture on a bulletin board with the title "What In The World Would You Do To Relax?"

The Bear's Toothache

This irresistible tale tells of a boy's efforts to relieve a bear of an aching tooth. After hearing the story, have each youngster take a turn standing at the front of the room holding a pillow that has a giant tooth cutout on it. Have him explain to the tooth fairy why this tooth is so large. Have him also compare the value of this giant tooth to that of a small human one. These soliloquies are likely to be precious, so capture them on videotape.

Pig Pig Rides

In his wild imaginings, Pig Pig drives a delivery truck, a racing car, a motorcycle, a train, and a rocket. Create a booklet of similar adventures from your students' imaginations. Ask each child to give an imaginative response to the question "What are you doing today?" Write his response on a sheet of art paper; then have him illustrate it. Bind the pages between tagboard covers. Label the cover "What are you doing today?" Delight your youngsters with other Pig Pig adventures: *Pig Pig Goes To Camp* and *Pig Pig Grows Up*.

Alligators Are Awful (And They Have Terrible Manners, Too)

(This book is out of print. Check your library.)

There's just no excuse for poor manners, as this book so colorfully points out. Read the book aloud. Then, using colored chalk, sketch a giant alligator with an opened mouth on the chalkboard. Draw giant teeth in the alligator's mouth so that there is a tooth in the upper jaw for each tooth in the lower jaw. As students recall each of the ill-mannered actions of an alligator, note it on a lower tooth. Then have students propose a more considerate alternative for each ill-mannered action. Note this recommendation on the corresponding tooth in the upper jaw of the sketched alligator.

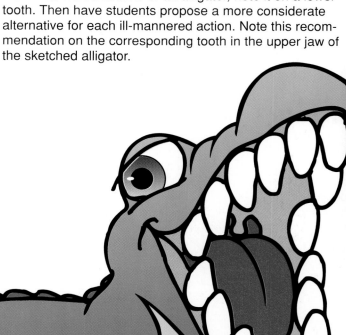

First Flight

Although the little boy in the story maintains his composure during his first flight, his bear companion runs the gamut of emotions before they reach their destination. This book is the perfect complement to an airport field trip. But if a trip is out of the question, prepare for departure from your classroom. Line up chairs in rows of four with an aisle down the middle to resemble airplane seating. Have each child give you, the head flight attendant, his boarding pass before taking his seat and stowing his luggage underneath the seat. Have selected students serve as assistant flight attendants as you serve a light snack during the quick flight. Encourage students to talk about what they see, feel, and hear during this imaginary flight.

The Bear's Bicycle

Written by Emilie Warren McLeod
Illustrated by David McPhail

The little boy in this story takes many of the necessary precautions to keep himself safe while riding his bike. But his teddy bear comes to life and embodies irresponsibility on wheels. Invite a local expert on bike safety to speak to your class. And, if possible, conduct a bicycle safety rodeo so that children can practice safe biking in a controlled instructional setting. Once safe biking practices have been discussed, award a bear-embellished ribbon to each child who pledges to implement safe biking practices.

Snow Lion

If it's sweltering where you are, *Snow Lion* may be a welcome wintry blast. Introduce the story by showing the students a red tote bag. Explain in animated fashion that your friend Lion said that you could show them the really cool stuff inside the bag. Then dump out the contents of the bag: a toothbrush and a comb. Pretend to be mystified; then begin reading the story aloud. You'll have piqued your students' interest before you even show the book's cover.

Lost!

Read this story to spark personal safety discussions. Have each child press a large bear-shaped sponge into a shallow pan of tempera paint before pressing the sponge once on newspaper to blot, and then onto construction paper. When the design is dry, have the artist cut loosely around it and use a marker to add facial details. As the student dictates, write one thing that a lost person needs to know on the back of the bear cutout. Suspend each of the bears by a ribbon from the ceiling.

Writing Out Loud With Robert Munsch

The stories Robert Munsch creates for children aren't merely written, they *evolve*. He begins by *telling* a story to children. As the children listen, they add details. Munsch incorporates these details into the next telling. He continues to modify the story in this way each time he tells it. After several years, a great story has evolved and Munsch puts it down on paper. Since children contribute to each "group composition," the stories that develop are completely contemporary and fabulously funny. Children solve their own problems and control their own worlds, making these extraordinary stories quite empowering for the readers. Encourage your youngsters to add their own creative touches to these stories, and before you know it— you'll all be writing out loud with Robert Munsch!

by Kim T. Griswell

Purple, Green And Yellow
Illustrated by Hélène Desputeaux
Annick Press Ltd.

Brigid loves markers. She loves brightly colored washable markers, smelly markers, even super-indelible-never-come-off markers! She draws such wonderful pictures that her mother declares, "Wow! My kid is an artist." Your budding artists will be ready to get their hands on markers after you share *Purple, Green And Yellow*. Have each child lie down on a length of bulletin-board paper. Trace her outline onto the paper. Provide lots of brightly colored markers, and encourage the child to fill her outline with vibrant designs similar to those Brigid colored in the book. Then have her cut out her outline. Post all of your students' artistic creations in the hall under the title "Wow! [Your name]'s Students Are Artists."

The Fire Station
Illustrated by Michael Martchenko
Annick Press Ltd.

Fire up your students' curiosity as you read about Michael and Sheila—two friends whose inquisitiveness leads them into a messy misadventure. Since Sheila's decision to sneak aboard the fire truck led to the friends being colored by smoke, use this book as a thought-provoking way to look at cause and effect. After reading ask questions to help your youngsters see the effects of Sheila's actions. Reproduce a class supply of "Think Safety!" on page 72. Have each student color, then cut out the fire engine and cause-and-effect pictures. After he matches each cause to each effect, have him glue each matching pair on the fire engine.

Angela's Airplane
Illustrated by Michael Martchenko
Annick Press Ltd.

When Angela's father takes her to the airport, something awful happens—*he* gets lost. Angela's search for him leads her inside an airplane, and into the cockpit. She finds the array of buttons so interesting, she can't resist pushing a few. What happens next is no surprise, but is sure to be exciting to little ones with lots of curiosity. After sharing this story, soar into pretend flight with a shape-matching twist! On poster board draw a simplified outline of an airplane instrument panel. Add detail to the panel by tracing around shape blocks. Set up a center with the completed instrument panel and enough shape blocks to match one to each shape on the panel. Instruct each child using the center to match a block to each shape. Your little pilots will be in great shape after logging time in this cockpit!

Stephanie's Ponytail
Illustrated by Michael Martchenko
Annick Press Ltd.

Stephanie is a trendsetter. No matter how she wears her hair to school, everyone else copies her hairstyle. In an outrageous conclusion, she turns the tables on her style-stealing peers. Stephanie's confidence shines in this outrageous spoof of youngsters who give in to peer pressure. After sharing the book, start some styling trends in your class. Give each student a construction-paper head shape. Provide yarn in a variety of colors, ribbon, rubber bands, scissors, and glue. Have each student create a hairstyle by gluing yarn to the head shape, then styling the yarn hair. Have her add a face that reflects whether the wearer is happy or unhappy with the hairstyle. Staple the completed student styles on a bulletin board titled "Room [room number]'s Styling Salon."

Moira's Birthday
Illustrated by Michael Martchenko
Annick Press Ltd.

What do you get when you add all the students from grade 1, grade 2, grade 3, grade 4, grade 5, grade 6, *aaaand* kindergarten? You get Moira's birthday party! And how much food do you need for that many hungry hooligans? You need *two hundred* pizzas and *two hundred* birthday cakes. *Moira's Birthday* is a math problem waiting to happen. After sharing the book with your youngsters, set up a math center with pizza and birthday-cake cutouts. To use the center, have students work to create simple addition and subtraction problems. Have each student who uses the center write the problems she creates on a sheet to turn in to you.

50 Below Zero
Illustrated by Michael Martchenko
Annick Press Ltd.

Brrrrr! It's colder than cold outside and Jason's sleepwalking father wanders into the snow wearing nothing but his pajamas. Jason dons layers of clothing, then heads out to find his dad before he turns into a frozen ice cube. How cold is "un-bear-ably" cold? Once you've shared Jason's shivery story, this simple science experiment will answer the question. Provide a bag of Gummy bears® and a gallon of lemonade, along with a class supply of small (unwaxed) paper cups and Popsicle® sticks. Give each student a paper cup. Have her use a permanent marker to write her name on the cup. Instruct her to drop a Gummy bear® into the cup, then rest a Popsicle® stick inside the cup. Fill all of your students' cups with lemonade. Take your class to the kitchen and place the cups in the school's freezer. Note the time. Every half hour or so, check to see if the lemonade has frozen. When you find the lemonade frozen, note the time. Help students calculate how long it took the lemonade to freeze; then invite your youngsters to warm up the outside of their cups with their hands, pull out the frozen pops, and enjoy their "beary" cold treats.

79

Name _____

Think Safety!

✂️ Cut.   Match each cause and effect.

🖍️ Color.   Glue.

Pfister's Pfabulous Pfriends

Meet Marcus Pfister—author, illustrator, graphic designer, sculptor, painter, and photographer. In addition to his popular Penguin Pete and Hopper series, Pfister has authored two international best-sellers—*The Rainbow Fish* and *The Christmas Star*. It might interest you to know that several of his books are available in French, Spanish, and German. Pfister lives in Berne, Switzerland, with his wife and sons.

From *Penguin Pete and Little Tim* by Marcus Pfister, published by North-South Books, Inc., New York. Copyright ©1994 by Nord-Süd Verlag AG, Gossau Zürich, Switzerland.

Follow Penguin Pete!

The five books in Marcus Pfister's Penguin Pete series are delightful read-alouds for a winter or penguin unit. Introduce your students to the irresistible, big-eyed penguin by reading aloud *Penguin Pete.* Then travel with Pete on an adventurous fishing trip in *Penguin Pete's New Friends*. In *Penguin Pete And Pat*, Pete meets an adorable girl penguin with a blue beak. Pete finds adventure and a new friend in *Penguin Pete, Ahoy!*, but settles down to family life in *Penguin Pete And Little Tim.*

Penguin Facts

In addition to precious art and appealing stories, the books in the Penguin Pete series provide the perfect opportunity for youngsters to learn some fine-feathered facts about penguins. Visually divide a chart into two columns. Label one column "Penguin Facts" and the second column "Book Title." After reading each book aloud, ask students to list the facts about penguins that they deduced from the story. Write the dictated facts on the chart along with the title of the story that provided that information.

Penguin Facts	Book Title
Penguins lay eggs.	Penguin Pete and Pat
Penguins eat fish.	Penguin Pete's New Friends
Penguins swim well.	Penguin Pete, Ahoy!

Penguin Pete And Pat

When yellow-beaked Pete arrives home from his travels with Walter Whale, all of his friends—including a blue-beaked penguin named Pat—greet him. A romance, a wedding, and an egg soon follow. To their surprise, when little Tim is born, he has a green beak! After reading *Penguin Pete And Pat* aloud, give youngsters an opportunity to make unique penguins. To make one, cut a large, black construction-paper oval to represent the penguin's body. Then glue on two smaller ovals to resemble flippers. Next glue a white oval to the penguin's body and two small, white ovals to the top to resemble eyes. Color the eyes with a black marker. Finally add two orange triangles to resemble webbed feet. Blend two primary colors of your choice on a tagboard triangle beak to create a new color; then glue the beak to the penguin project.

Catherine V. Herber—PreK–3, Highland Preschool
Raleigh, NC

The Rainbow Fish

In this enchanting tale, the Rainbow Fish learns about sharing, caring, and the beauty that comes from within. A discussion of these values fits swimmingly with a reading of *The Rainbow Fish*. To extend the beauty of the story, choose from the following suggested activities:

Fancy Fish

These rainbow fish with their shimmering, silver scales will create a dazzling display. To make a rainbow fish, trace the fish pattern (page 83) onto a colored piece of construction paper; then cut it out. Paint the fish with several colors of tempera paint, swirling and mixing the colors for a unique effect. Sprinkle glitter over the wet paint and press on silver wrapping-paper scales. When dry, mount the fish onto a board along with several bulletin-board-paper waves.

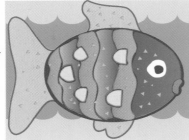

Michelle Allen
Northwest Elementary
Ankeny, IA

A Song About Sharing

After reading *The Rainbow Fish*, sing the first two verses of the song below. Then ask each child to imagine that he is the Rainbow Fish. Would he share his scales? Why or why not? Follow up the discussion by singing the song again, including the last verse if desired.

(sung to the tune of "The Muffin Man")
Have you heard of the Rainbow Fish,
The Rainbow Fish, the Rainbow Fish?
Have you heard of the Rainbow Fish?
He wouldn't share his scales.

If you were the Rainbow Fish,
The Rainbow Fish, the Rainbow Fish;
If you were the Rainbow Fish,
Would you share your scales?

If I were the Rainbow Fish,
The Rainbow Fish, the Rainbow Fish;
If I were the Rainbow Fish,
YES! I'd share my scales.

Adapted from an idea by Nell Nunn
Special Education
Ferson Creek School
St. Charles, IL

Special Scales

Wouldn't it be special if every child could have a sparkling, silver scale of her own? Before reading *The Rainbow Fish* aloud, safety-pin large sequins to a stuffed-toy fish or fish puppet. (A glittering bluefish puppet is available from Demco's Kids & Things™. Call 1-800-356-1200 and ask for item 171-4525 for the puppet or item 171-5583 for the book and puppet set.) Read the story aloud while animating the puppet; then pin one sequin scale to each child's shirt. These special scales will be a visual reminder to youngsters to share throughout the day.

Keitha-Lynn Stewart
Little Kids Day Care
Sissonville, WV

Creative Sharing

After viewing this cooperative art project, everyone will want to get their hands on *The Rainbow Fish*. Enlarge the fish pattern on page 83 onto white poster board; then cut out the fish. Paint the fins and head of the fish to resemble Pfister's Rainbow Fish, leaving the center of the fish white. Using paint in various shades of blue, green, and purple, have each child press his handprints onto the center of the fish. Be sure to add a foil wrapping-paper scale. When the project is dry, consider displaying it in your school or community library.

Brenda Hume, Summerville, SC

More Pfister Fiction
Published by North-South Books

Hopper
Hopper Hunts For Spring
Hang On, Hopper!

Dazzle The Dinosaur
The Christmas Star

From *Penguin Pete and Little Tim* by Marcus Pfister, published by North-South Books, Inc., New York.
Copyright ©1994 by Nord-Süd Verlag AG, Gossau Zürich, Switzerland.

"Why Should I Waste A Perfectly Good Story On You?"

Patricia Polacco And Her Books

Forty-some years ago, Patricia Polacco's grandmother strolled around an enormous rock in her front yard. "Do you want to know how this got here?" she asked. Patricia looked at the rock and said, "Well, Bubee, that's a rock." "Well, if a rock is all you can see, what a pity! It means you have no imagination. If you have no imagination, why should I waste a perfectly good story on you?" So Patricia said, "Hasn't it always been there?" During the conversation that ensued, Patricia's grandmother told her the story of a falling star which was the inspiration for *Meteor!,* Patricia's first book.

Even though her grandmother died before Patricia's fifth birthday, her storytelling (and that of other family members, including her dad) had a profound effect on Patricia. Much of Patricia's writing is based on experiences she had on her grandmother's farm in Union City, Michigan. After her grandmother's death, Patricia and her family moved to Oakland, California, to a neighborhood characterized by a mix of cultures, races, and religions. It was there that she met her lifelong friend Stewart Washington. *Chicken Sunday* is Patricia's book about Stewart's family.

In Patricia's family, when a child was about to read, it was customary to put a drop of honey on the cover of the book. The message that this symbolized was that, like honey, knowledge is sweet. Like the bee from which the honey came, knowledge may be illusive. But if you chase it through the pages of books, it will finally be yours. For Patricia, the chase was an especially difficult one, since she had undiagnosed learning disabilities. When she was 14, a teacher discovered this well-guarded secret and paid for Patricia to have twice-weekly sessions with a reading specialist. Years later, Patricia's high school English teacher ridiculed her spelling, but admitted, "...you *do* tell a good story!" The overwhelming majority of people who have read her books can't testify as to her poor spelling, but most wholeheartedly agree that she definitely tells a good story.

From JUST PLAIN FANCY by Patricia Polacco. Copyright ©1990 by Patricia Polacco. Used by permission of Bantam Books, a division of Random House, Inc.

Meteor!

Published by G. P. Putnam

It seems appropriate that Patricia Polacco's version of her grandmother's falling-star story became her first children's book. At the age of 41, Patricia seemed to fall from nowhere smack-dab into the mainstream of children's literature. Like the rock around which *Meteor!* pivots, Patricia Polacco is a source of wonder. Reading *Meteor!* is a great way to introduce your youngsters to this author and her work.

After reading the story aloud, ask parents to help their youngsters make imitation meteorites. To get the creative juices flowing, mention that rocks, play dough, rhinestones, glitter, and paint are but a few of the materials that may be used to create imitation meteorites. Set aside a specific day as the day for all meteorites to be sent to school. On that special day, collect the meteorites at the door and arrange them in a special area. Consider roping off the area and spotlighting the student-made meteorites. Unveil your remarkable collection of magnificent meteorites and serve meteor popcorn and meteor lemonade as students discuss their creations.

Pam Warren—Gr. K
DeSoto Trail Elementary
Tallahassee, FL

Thunder Cake

Published by Philomel Books

Thunder Cake is Patricia Polacco's story about the way her grandmother taught her to face and overcome her fear of thunder. Plan to read the story on a rainy day and place the ingredients for *Thunder Cake* (see the recipe at the back of the book) at different locations around your classroom. Discuss thunder, lightning, and rain with your youngsters. If desired, read excerpts from Seymour Simon's *Storms* (published by Mulberry Books) or Franklyn M. Branley's *Flash, Crash, Rumble, And Roll* (published by Harper Trophy) to clarify what happens during a storm. Then read *Thunder Cake*. Each time the characters in the story gather an ingredient, lead your youngsters to the spot where that ingredient had previously been placed and take the ingredient to the area where you'll be mixing the cake batter. Flash the lights whenever lightning is mentioned in the story; then stomp your feet to imitate the thunder. Count the time between the lightning and thunder, just as they do in the book. When all the ingredients have been gathered, mix and bake the Thunder Cake according to the directions at the back of the book.

Kimberle Suzan Byrd—Preschool
Mayflower Preschool
Grand Rapids, MI

Just Plain Fancy

Published by Bantam Books

Just Plain Fancy is a heartwarming story about an Amish girl, her family, and a fancy egg. The egg hatches into a fancy chick that grows into a truly fancy bird. After reading *Just Plain Fancy* to your students, guide them in making beautiful paper peacocks. To make a peacock, cut purple paper into a shape similar to that of a peacock's head and neck. Glue the purple cutout in the center near the bottom of a sheet of art paper. Use oval-shaped sponges dipped in green paint to nearly cover the white paper with prints. Sponge paint the center of each oval with a smaller oval-shaped sponge dipped in blue paint. Sponge paint the center of each blue oval with a smaller round sponge dipped in black paint. To complete the peacock, paint a black dot on the purple cutout for its eye.

Jayne M. Gammons—Gr. K-1
Oak Grove Elementary
Durham, NC

The Keeping Quilt

Published by Simon And Schuster Books For Young Readers

Patricia Polacco's Great-Gramma Anna came to America with her Russian family. To preserve the memories of the people that they had left behind, Anna's mother made a quilt using fabric from Anna's babushka (scarf) and also pieces of clothing which belonged to their relatives in "back-home" Russia. Over the years, the quilt became an important part of family celebrations.

Before reading *The Keeping Quilt,* discuss family relationships and family heirlooms. Show students a real quilt. If possible, have a quilter explain to students how quilts are made. After reading the story, have children make quiltlike cards to give to relatives for special occasions such as Mother's Day, Father's Day, or Grandparents Day. Assist each student in folding a sheet of construction paper in half (to 6" x 9"); then help him fold it in a trifold manner (to 3" x 6"). Fold the paper in half once more, creating roughly a three-inch square. Have each youngster unfold his paper. From an assortment of two-inch wallpaper squares, have each student select 12 squares and glue them to the sections of his paper. Once more have each youngster fold his paper in half to resemble a greeting card and write a message inside the card. Attach a dated copy of the poem (below) opposite the handwritten message and include a child-drawn picture of the family.

Kimberle Suzan Byrd—Preschool
Mayflower Preschool
Grand Rapids, MI

After reading *The Keeping Quilt,* help youngsters portray some of their best family memories. Give each child a personalized six-inch square of construction paper. Instruct him to discuss with his family things or happenings that have long been special to the family. Based on this discussion, encourage the child to draw a picture on his square that is symbolic of this special thing or event. As students return their squares to school, attach the squares to a fabric-covered bulletin board to resemble a quilt. Give each youngster an opportunity to explain the significance of his drawing to his classmates. Continue to add to the bulletin board student-illustrated squares that symbolize special school days and activities. Invite others to your classroom so that your youngsters will have lots of opportunities to tell about their keeping quilt.

Patricia Leary Burns—Gr. Jr. K
Oakfield-Alabama Elementary
Oakfield, NY

Here's another way to follow up a reading of *The Keeping Quilt.* Have each child contribute (with parental permission) an eight-inch square of fabric from something that has been especially meaningful to him. One child may want to contribute a square of fabric from a baby blanket, while others may contribute squares from special shirts or worn-out pajamas. Have each child write his name on his fabric square using a fabric pen. If desired, allow students to decorate their squares with fabric paints, ribbons, or other supplies. Locate a group of senior citizens who are willing to make your students' squares into a quilt. Display your students' keeping quilt in the classroom; then donate it to an organization that will give it to someone who can use the quilt.

Mary Jane Simpson
Barksdale Elementary
Conyers, GA

> A family's like a patchwork quilt,
> With kindness gently sewn.
> Each piece is an original,
> With beauty of its own.
> With threads of warmth and happiness,
> It's tightly stitched together
> To last in love through the years.
> A family is forever.

1st fold 2nd fold 3rd fold

Happy Mother's Day! Love, Ben

Babushka's Doll

Published by Simon & Schuster

After reading aloud *Babushka's Doll*, your students will certainly be able to discuss just how naughty the doll really was. In a more positive vein, ask them to think of ways to be helpful at school and at home. Have each child choose his favorite way to be helpful. As he dictates, write his comments on a speech balloon cutout. Then have each child decorate a paper plate to resemble the face of Babushka's doll. To make the doll's bonnet, have each child tear a free-form tagboard shape and glue on fabric squares to cover it. Staple the bonnet to the doll's paper-plate face. Display each doll with the speech balloon of its creator.

I can be helpful by always having something nice to say.

Harriet Velevis—Pre/K
Jewish Community Center Preschool
Dallas, TX

After you've read *Babushka's Doll* to your students, seize the opportunity to encourage youngsters to treat people the way they would want to be treated. Then show the students a drawing of Babushka's doll or a puppet or doll that looks similar. Explain that the picture, puppet, or doll will be used to signal that students need to evaluate their behaviors and act accordingly. When the doll is moved from its usual perch, that is the signal for students to quiet down or work more cooperatively.

Concetta Castelluzzo and Jacqueline DeBolt
Penn Yan Central School Buddy Bear Team
Penn Yan, NY

Rechenka's Eggs

Published by Philomel Books

Patricia Polacco's relatives are from the Ukraine and the Georgian provinces in Russia where the delicate art of painting eggs originated. Thanks in part to her Babushka (grandmother) who taught her this traditional art, she too is talented in the art of Ukrainian egg painting, called *pysanky*. Egg painting is the subject of the book *Rechenka's Eggs*. Reading Rainbow featured *Rechenka's Eggs* during one of its programs. Following a reading of the story during the program, Polacco demonstrated the art of egg painting. To acquaint your students with *Rechenka's Eggs* or to introduce your students to the author and/or pysanky, play the Reading Rainbow videotape for your students. If a copy is unavailable from your school librarian, call GPN at 1-800-228-4630 to obtain ordering information. (You may also want to inquire about purchasing a copy of the Reading Rainbow program containing Polacco's *Mrs. Katz And Tush*.)

Inspired by the beautifully painted eggs in *Rechenka's Eggs*, your youngsters will be delighted to make these dazzling egg cutouts. To begin, draw or trace an egg shape onto poster board or tagboard. Using a brush and a mixture of equal parts of vinegar and water, wet the entire egg shape. Then place a tissue-paper square onto the poster board, and brush over it with the liquid. Continue placing additional tissue-paper squares on the wet surface until the egg shape is entirely covered. Allow the surface of the project to dry completely. Then brush off the squares. Students will be pleased to see the bright outcome of their uniquely dyed eggs.

Debbie Newsome
Dolvin Elementary School
Alpharetta, GA

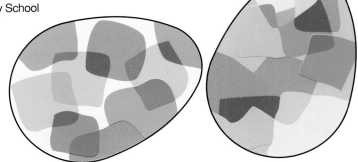

Chicken Sunday

Published by Philomel Books

When Patricia was four years old, her grandmother died. Shortly thereafter she and her mom moved to Oakland, California. It was there that she was befriended by an African-American family that included Eula Mae Walker and her grandsons, Stewart and Winston Washington. To this day, Patricia claims Stewart as her best friend. In Patricia's Easter story, *Chicken Sunday*, students can see Eula Mae, Stewart, Winston, and Patricia. After reading aloud and discussing the story, you may want to show students the portion of the *Rechenka's Eggs* Reading Rainbow program that shows the author making pysanky eggs. (See *Rechenka's Eggs* for more information.) Then assist your youngsters in decorating egg cutouts to resemble Ukrainian eggs. Have students color firmly, creating designs on egg shapes cut from art paper. Then instruct each student to use a large brush and black watercolor paint to cover the entire cutout.

Jayne Gammons—Grs. K-1
Oak Grove Elementary
Durham, NC

Other Books By Patricia Polacco

Appelemando's Dreams • *Babushka Baba Yaga* • *The Bee Tree* • *Uncle Vova's Tree* •
Picnic At Mudsock Meadow • *Mrs. Katz And Tush*

Reading With Raffi!

Using Raffi's Songs-To-Read In Your Classroom

Dear Teachers,

It's a delight for me to be able to speak to you through the pages of *The Mailbox®*, and to learn that, through my work, I am a regular visitor in your classrooms.

I have always believed that music can be a natural bridge between speaking and reading. I am honored that so many of you are using my songs and books to help bring your students to literacy, and are willing to take the time to share your ideas with other professionals.

My own work with children has brought me joy, satisfaction, and an ongoing feeling of wonder and delight. May your work reward you in all the same ways.

Thank you,

Raffi ♡

Jamal   Shawn

Like Me And You
Illustrated by Lillian Hoban
Published by
Crown Books For Young Readers

This treasure of a book is a wonderful choice to use at the beginning of the year when students are just getting to know each other. Young readers will sing and say the names of children around the world as they are illustrated mailing letters to one another. After sharing the book with your children, discuss each of your students' names. When appropriate, talk about the culture from which each child's family originated. Invite parents from other cultures to visit your class to share information about their places of origin.

Down By The Bay

Illustrated by Nadine Bernard Westcott
Published by Crown Books For Young Readers

When he's in concert, Raffi sometimes jokes that the audience won't let him leave until he has sung this song with them! In this book, two friends use their imaginations and rhyme to create some of the silliest scenes you have ever laid eyes on! Share *Down By The Bay* with your children. After reading and discussing the book, teach the tune to your children and sing the book. Then announce that you are all going on an imaginary trip to the bay. Proceed by singing the song, inserting a different child's name and corresponding rhyming word each time. (If you can't think of real rhyming words—make them up!)

Jennifer Kreskai—Age 3-Gr. K, Kid's Land Inc.
South Bend, IN

Youngsters will be eager to create outlandish art projects to accompany their wild imaginings. Have each child choose a pair of rhyming words from *Down By The Bay* or a pair that he thought of on his own. Then provide a variety of art supplies and have each child illustrate his chosen rhyme. For example, a child could use a bingo marker to make polka dots on the tail of a whale cutout, or use fabric scraps to make a colorful bow tie for a construction-paper fly. Display the finished projects; then sing a verse of the song for each one.

Dawn Hurley, CUMC Child Care Center, Bethel Park, PA

After you've ventured "down by the bay, where the watermelons grow," a seed search makes a wonderful thematic extension into math. In advance, cut a large semicircle from poster board and color it to resemble a slice of watermelon. Program the cutout as shown. Then give each child a real watermelon wedge. Ask her to pick out all of the seeds and place them on a paper towel. After rinsing and drying the seeds, have each child count her seeds; then write her name on the graph to represent the number of seeds that she has. Encourage each child to help decorate the graph by gluing her seeds around the edges. When the graph is complete, discuss the results with your students.

Kim Gray, Warren Elementary School, Alvaton, KY

Baby Beluga
Illustrated by Ashley Wolff
Published by Crown Books For Young Readers

According to Raffi's experience, "Children love this song because it is a bright and tuneful love song for a baby whale. Hearing it and singing it is enough for them; they don't need to be told that it's trying to teach them anything." But a child who grows up with this song, says Raffi, is likely to become an adult who will—at the very least—be sensitive to reports about the fatal pollution of the water belugas live in. After sharing this book and song with your children, choose one (or both) of the following suggestions to make a whale-related art project.

Water-Spouting Beluga

Trace or draw a beluga on white construction paper; then cut it out. Glue the beluga onto a large sheet of blue construction paper. Use crayons to draw an ocean scene around the beluga. On another sheet of white paper, use watercolor paint to paint a long waterspout. Cut out the spout and glue it onto a craft stick or long pipe cleaner. Cut a slit near the top of the beluga's head. Slide the craft stick or pipe cleaner into the slit so that the waterspout appears to come from the beluga. As you read the story again, children can move the water-spout up and down.

Jennifer Barton—Gr. K, Elizabeth Green School, Newington, CT

Whale Watching

Display pictures of various types of whales. Encourage students to carefully study the pictures and discuss the differences among all of the whales. Then give each child (or small group of children) a long length of bulletin-board paper that has been folded in half vertically. Direct each child to draw the whale of his choice on the paper, adding crayon details as desired. Assist children in cutting out a double thickness of their whales. Staple around the outline of the cutouts, leaving an opening at the bottom. Have each child gently stuff his whale with newspaper or plastic grocery bags. Staple the whales on a ocean bulletin-board background. Mount a label near each individual whale.

Carol Steiner—Gr. K, Jackson Elementary School
Green Bay, WI

One Light, One Sun
Illustrated by Eugenie Fernandes
Published by Crown Books For Young Readers

This warm and wonderful ballad was written by Raffi to convey that all people, no matter how different, have very much in common. We have one light and one sun—enough for everyone! After sharing the book with your students, sing the song together. Encourage children to discuss the meaning of the story and song. Then have each child or small group of children use representations of items in the story to make a mobile. (Depending on the art techniques you choose to use, you might like to work on these mobiles in more than one sitting.) Here's one way to make a mobile: Cut a sun shape from construction paper. Glue on orange and yellow yarn to decorate the sun. Color or paint a construction-paper circle to resemble the world. Glue construction-paper shapes and scraps together to make a house. Cut out a construction-paper heart and decorate it with pink and red tissue paper and glitter. When the projects are dry, use yarn to hang them from a hanger. Display each mobile as a reminder of Raffi's song and the message that it carries.

Carmen Carpenter, Highland Preschool, Raleigh, NC

Five Little Ducks

Illustrated by Jose Aruego and Ariane Dewey
Published by Crown Books For Young Readers

In one version or another, this story has probably entered almost every kindergarten classroom. Your little ones are bound to love Raffi's version of the story with its delightful surprise ending. In advance, prepare five construction-paper duck cutouts. Make stick puppets by taping a craft stick to the back of each cutout. Then read the story aloud. After discussing the story, *sing* the story together. Then give each of the five duck puppets to different children. Have the children (ducks) stand side by side while the class sings the song. As each duck wanders off—according to the song's lyrics—have her squat down. When it's time for the wandering ducks to come back, direct each duck to take the hand of a classmate to come waddling back with her as her duckling. When the song is over, have the adult ducks give their puppets to the ducklings. Sing the song until everyone has had a turn to be a duck. But be forewarned—Raffi says that sometimes, it's hard to stop quacking once you start!

Terri Nix—Gr. K, Brauchle Elementary School,
San Antonio, TX

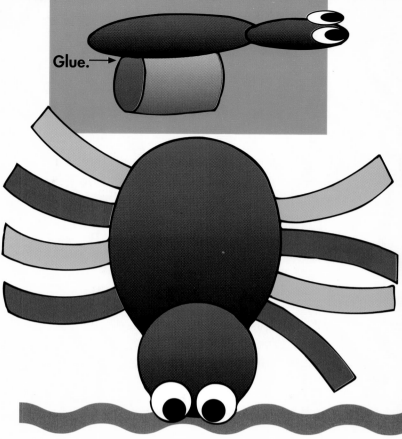

Glue.

Pam Crane

Spider On The Floor

Words and Music by Bill Russell
Illustrated by True Kelley
Published by Crown Books For Young Readers

Bill Russell taught Raffi this silly, spidery rhyming song that will entice even your most reluctant readers. After reading the book aloud, give each child a plastic spider ring or a small pom-pom. As you read the book aloud a second time, have each child move his spider on his own body according to the text.

Pamela Rose, St. Paul Lutheran Preschool, Bonduel, WI

Using Raffi's *Spider On The Floor* is one of the rare times that creepy crawlies will be welcome at storytime! Have each child make a spider from construction-paper pieces and wiggle eyes. Glue a construction-paper loop to the back of each spider to make a finger puppet. Ask each child to bring his finger puppet to storytime and manipulate his spider as you read the story aloud. Afterward ask each child to think of more body parts. Then call out a child's name. Using the format in the book, the child will say, "There's a spider on my [elbow], on my [elbow]." The other children move their spiders to the indicated body part. Then the child who chose that body part says, "But he jumps off!" Call out another child's name, continuing in the same manner until each child has had a turn to choose a body part.

Randalyn Larson—Gr. K, Memorial School,
Jackson, MI

A Wild Literature Rumpus

Sendak stories aren't for the faint of heart. They demand to be read and interpreted with gusto and glee. And judging by the ideas we received from your colleagues, classroom activities related to Sendak books are often ingeniously imaginative and sometimes downright aerobic! Clear the floor and kick up your heels. It's wild rumpus time!

Maurice Sendak, born in Brooklyn in 1928, was a frail and delicate boy. During a long series of childhood illnesses, he was enthralled by his father's imaginative storytelling sessions. Since Sendak found making friends difficult, he spent much of his time drawing pictures. For his ninth birthday, his sister gave him his first real book, *The Prince And The Pauper.* It was with this gift that his passion for books and bookmaking began.

One of his unpublished works, *Where The Wild Horses Are,* was the original fantasy behind *Where The Wild Things Are.* Because he felt he couldn't draw horses well, Sendak tried lots of different animals in the title. Finally, after deciding that "things" could be sufficiently frightening, he began to develop the story.

Where The Wild Things Are, the 1964 Caldecott Medal winner, launched the frail little boy from Brooklyn into an art and writing career that's nothing short of a dream come true.

Where The Wild Things Are
Published by HarperCollins Children's Books

Your youngsters can let their imaginations run rampant as they design three-dimensional "wild things." Start by having children reexamine the pictures of the wild things in *Where The Wild Things Are*. Then provide each youngster with a lump of clay, and encourage him to mold it into an original wild thing. As the student dictates a description of his finished masterpiece, write it on a folded self-standing card. In a display case or on a tabletop, exhibit each student's clay creation with its description card.

Kimberle Suzan Byrd—Preschool
Mayflower Preschool
Grand Rapids, MI

My wild thing is BIG, with BIG horns and BIG teeth.

Pam Crane

Classroom guests can take an imaginary journey to where the wild things are and find themselves taking an active role in a wild rumpus. First suspend leaf cutouts from the ceiling on crepe-paper streamers to set the stage for this dramatization of *Where The Wild Things Are*. Then cover a small table with a cloth and place a plant on it. Place a stuffed toy dog near the table. Have students rehearse their assigned parts. Explain that when it's time for the final production to begin, designated students will hand out noisemakers to the people in the audience. Also explain that you (or a parent volunteer) will cue the audience when it's time to create a commotion with their noisemakers. During your practice session(s) use a noisemaker at the appropriate points in the story so that students will become accustomed to the noise. And have students practice getting people from the audience to participate in the wild rumpus. Soon it will be time to say, "Lights, camera, action!"

Cathie Pesa
Paul C. Bunn School
Youngstown, OH

Expect a display of these patchwork wild things to be quite the conversation piece. After reading *Where The Wild Things Are,* divide students into small groups and provide art supplies for each group. Within each group, assign a child a wild thing body part to render. After each child is done, instruct the members of each group to glue the parts together to make a wild thing. Invite each group to name its creature before displaying it for all to enjoy.

Cathy Albracht—Gr. K
Christ The King School
Omaha, NE

These marvelous wild-thing masks will add to the excitement of a classroom wild rumpus. To prepare for this activity, cut eyeholes from a thin paper plate for each student. With the paper plate as a base for a mask, have each student decorate the back of his plate using markers, crayons, yarn, sequins, feathers, construction paper, and/or glue to resemble the face of a truly unusual wild thing. Attach yarn or ribbon to the sides of each decorated plate for tying the mask in place. If desired, provide students with rhythm instruments so that they can create lots of noise during their wild rumpus. "Let the wild rumpus begin!"

Brenda Hume—Child Development Teacher, Sangaree Elementary School Summerville, SC

If your youngsters are ready and willing to act out *Where The Wild Things Are,* collect a few old pillowcases to spark lots of creative fun. Positioning the opening of a pillowcase so that it will be the bottom of the costume, cut a hole for the child's face near the closed or upper end. Also cut armholes that are approximately 10" to 15" below the closed end. (For the best results, consider having a volunteer place the pillowcase over his head so that you can quickly mark the openings for the first costume. Then use these markings as a pattern for the remainder of the pillowcases.) To make ears, stuff each of the upper corners with fiberfill, gather it below the stuffing, and secure it with a rubber band. For a Max costume, use a permanent marker to draw whiskers near the facial opening of a pillowcase. For each wild thing costume, provide a working surface by placing a large piece of cardboard in a prepared pillowcase. Then have students use craft glue to attach feathers, ribbons, construction paper, fabric, or fur scraps to create a wild thing. When the costumes are thoroughly dry, have students don them and dramatize the story as you reread it aloud.

Diann M. Kroos—Preschool, SRI/St. Elizabeth Child Development Center, Lincoln, NE

○ shake your head

○ stomp your feet

○ rock from side to side

○ dance around

Are you ready for a wild rumpus in your room? Then follow up a reading of *Where The Wild Things Are* with this activity. In preparation for this game, have the children brainstorm a list of actions. Note the specified actions on chart paper accompanied by rebus word pictures. Review the rebus pictures and accompanying action descriptions with students. Then select one child to be the first queen (or king) of the wild things. Place a paper crown on that student's head. Explain that the remaining students are to pretend to be wild things that will do the bidding of the queen (or king). Referring to the list on the chart, have the crowned student command the wild things to perform a selected action. To stop the action after a few seconds, have the monarch raise her hand. To continue play, the queen passes her crown to another student who takes her place and gives the next command.

Randi Larson—Gr. K, Memorial School, Jackson, MI

If, during the waning months of school, your kindergartners are really into *Where The Wild Things Are,* you have the perfect opportunity to smooth their transition into first grade. After reading aloud *Where The Wild Things Are,* have each student cut a wild thing's body from a large sheet of construction paper. Provide miscellaneous art supplies, and ask that each student uniquely decorate his wild thing. Pair each of your students with a first grader who can tell him about the things he has to look forward to next year. After they have talked for a while, have the first grader in each pair write what the younger student says that he is most anticipating about first grade. On a bulletin board labeled "We're Wild About Going To First Grade," display each student's wild thing and the comments he made to his first-grade companion.

Randi Larson—Gr. K

Chicken Soup With Rice: A Book Of Months

Published by HarperCollins Children's Books

Get each new month off to a great start with the corresponding verse from Maurice Sendak's *Chicken Soup With Rice: A Book Of Months*. Copy each month's verse onto a separate sheet of chart paper, including a credit line. Then, at the start of each new month, read the corresponding verse aloud to your students. Discuss the seasonal elements that Sendak mentions. Provide miscellaneous art supplies, and encourage each youngster to make one decorated cutout related to each month's verse. Embellish the margins of the chart paper by attaching the students' projects.

Cindy Stefanick—Gr. K/1 Resource, Quinsigamond School
Uxbridge, MA

One of the best ways to get your students into the spirit of *Chicken Soup With Rice: A Book Of Months*, is by serving some chicken soup with rice. Begin by reading aloud the book. Then have students help you prepare the tasty dish according to a favorite recipe or straight from a can. When everyone has a warm bowlful of chicken soup with rice, treat them even further by showing the video titled *The Maurice Sendak Library*. This video includes Carole King's renditions of "Chicken Soup With Rice," "Alligators All Around," "Pierre," and "One Was Johnny." Sendak fans will also enjoy this tape's adaptations of *Where The Wild Things Are* and *In The Night Kitchen*.

Cindy Stefanick—Gr. K/1 Resource
Diann M. Kroos—Preschool
SRI/St. Elizabeth Child Development Center
Lincoln, NE

Use *Chicken Soup With Rice: A Book Of Months* as the basis for an end-of-the-year program. If you have taught each month's verse during the corresponding month of the school year, youngsters will have to learn very little new material, and there will be very little need for practice. Instruct each student to say the verse for his birth month, using simple props that you've gathered or assembled quickly. For participants who were born in September, for example, glue colored crocodile head cutouts onto paint stirring sticks, and have students use them as masks. For participants who were born in May, provide chefs' hats (or similar) and wooden spoons. This production may be sung rather than chorally spoken, if desired. To produce the musical version, have your students sing the verses accompanied by Carole King's recording of "Chicken Soup With Rice" from her audiocassette *Really Rosie*.

Katie Baily—Gr. K, Edgewood School, Bristol, CT

Pierre: A Cautionary Tale In Five Chapters And A Prologue

Published by HarperCollins Children's Books

In *Pierre: A Cautionary Tale In Five Chapters And A Prologue*, Maurice Sendak beautifully shows how quickly a change of perspective can alter what appears to be an absolutely unshakable attitude. Read the story to your youngsters; then bring the book alive by having students dramatize Carole King's rendition of "Pierre" from her audiocassette *Really Rosie*. To costume the student playing Pierre, provide clothing and props similar to those in the book's illustrations. To outfit the other students, use adult clothing. For the lion, use an eyebrow pencil to draw whiskers on the actor's face. If your students dramatize this story for an end-of-the-year program, brace yourself for the encore requests.

Pam Warren—Gr. K, DeSoto Trail Elementary, Tallahassee, FL

Very Far Away

Published by HarperCollins Children's Books

"I need to get out of here and go very far away!" That's the kind of feeling Martin found he shared with some interesting animal acquaintances in *Very Far Away*. But when Martin and his friends got to "very far away," they found their needs for solitude were incompatible. Discuss what running away actually accomplished for Martin. Bring out the fact that even though most of us feel a need to break out of our usual routines every now and then, we usually only need a little time away before we feel ready to face the things we originally wanted to escape. Ask your youngsters to describe their personal versions of "very far away." Find out if your youngsters have ever felt that they'd like to get very far away from school. Have your students decorate and supply an area that is designed specifically for getting away from it all—right in your classroom.

Pam Warren—Gr. K

Alligators All Around: An Alphabet

Published by HarperCollins Children's Books

Alligators are the main characters in this alphabet book full of letter-associated activities. After sharing *Alligators All Around: An Alphabet* with students, explain that together you're going to make an alphabet book, but that it will feature another type of animal. Give students an opportunity to brainstorm potential animal characters to serve as the main characters in the student-published book. Have each student vote for one of the suggested animals. If desired, record the responses in graph form. Once the animal of choice has been determined, assign each student an alphabet letter (or letters). Provide him with a large sheet of art paper for illustrating his animal in action with an object (or objects) that begins with the assigned letter. Label each student's page with his assigned letter and his brief description of the illustration. Collect the pages from the students, and ask that they help you put the pages in the proper sequence. Staple the sequenced pages between student-decorated covers; then read this newly published book to its authors.

Kelly A. Wong, Berlyn School, Ontario, CA

p Jackson planting petunias in a pot

One Was Johnny: A Counting Book

Published by HarperCollins Children's Books

Johnny, who lived all by himself, got interrupted by all kinds of creatures. After reading aloud *One Was Johnny: A Counting Book,* have your youngsters choose a teacher, the principal, or other popular person or character to substitute for Johnny in a remake of this story. Photocopy a picture of the person who will be the new main character. Prepare the photocopied picture for flannelboard use by backing it with felt. Have students suggest animals to substitute for the rat, cat, dog, turtle, monkey, blackbird, tiger, and robber in the story. Assign one of the new characters to each of several small student groups, asking the group to locate a magazine picture of that creature that is suitable for flannelboard use. Cut out these pictures and back them with felt. Re-read the text of the story, changing it to reflect students' substitutions. Have students add each flannelboard character to the display as it is mentioned in the story and remove it from the flannelboard as indicated by the modified text.

Kelly A. Wong, Berlyn School, Ontario, CA

In The Night Kitchen

Published by HarperCollins Children's Books

Maurice Sendak drew upon his childhood memories of a bakery advertisement as the inspiration for *In The Night Kitchen.* The ad, which read "We Bake While You Sleep!", taunted him. He imagined what it must be like to romp around all night in such a yummy place. Preview *In The Night Kitchen* before reading it aloud to your youngsters. Since this book contains nudity, it may not be appropriate for all groups.

After reading this story, have youngsters help you make a large batch of stiff bread or play dough. Give each child about a cup of dough and have him shape it into all sorts of things including a plane (like Mickey's) or cakes and bakery items. If desired, arrange to take youngsters to a bakery so that they can experience bakery sights, sounds, and tastes firsthand.

JoAnn Elliott, Eagle Bridge, NY

Other Books By Maurice Sendak

Hector Protector And As I Went Over The Water:
 Two Nursery Rhymes
Kenny's Window
Maurice Sendak's Really Rosie
Outside Over There
The Sign On Rosie's Door
We Are All In The Dumps With Jack And Guy:
 Two Nursery Rhymes

Seriously Seuss

The good doctor said, "You can't kid kids." But you don't have to be a kid to see that each of Dr. Seuss's characters and plots stands as a testament to the seriousness with which he took his writing. He was quoted as saying that to finish a sixty-page book, he might write a thousand pages. His overwhelming success is due largely to the fact that he worked slavishly over most of his stories—writing, rewriting, and perfecting each one.

Perhaps the most incredible experience Theodor Seuss Geisel had as a student was in his first high-school art class. The teacher called him aside at the end of the class and told him he would never learn to draw. She recommended that he not return to class. In a 1965 *Woman's Day* interview, he was quoted as saying, "I really can't draw at all, not in the artistic sense."

Years later, Geisel quit working on his doctorate degree to become a cartoonist. Knowing that his father had always wanted to see Dr. in front of his name, he assumed the pseudonym Dr. Seuss. Precociously he explained that he figured this decision saved his father about ten thousand dollars.

Dr. Seuss, a white-bearded fellow who tooled around California in his later years in a car bearing the license plate GRINCH, died in September 1991. But he had continued to produce children's books right up until his death, despite the fact that he was 87 years old. In all, he wrote 47 children's books, of which at least 200 million copies have been sold. His books are published in 20 different languages and sold worldwide. Theodor Seuss Geisel is considered by many to be the leading children's author of the twentieth century.

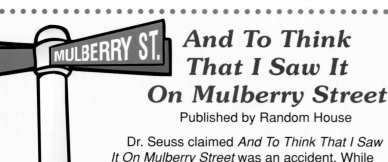

And To Think That I Saw It On Mulberry Street

Published by Random House

Dr. Seuss claimed *And To Think That I Saw It On Mulberry Street* was an accident. While crossing the Atlantic aboard a ship, he amused himself by writing his first children's book to the rhythmic hum of the engine. Later he drew the illustrations to accompany the story. Dr. Seuss's debut into the realm of children's literature met with 29 rejections from potential publishers. In 1937, Dr. Seuss brought his first book to the world, and you can bring it to your youngsters.

As the first and last parts of *And To Think That I Saw It On Mulberry Street* indicate, Marco is prone to telling outlandish tales. Read the book aloud to your youngsters; then discuss with them the way Marco imagined ordinary things into extraordinary things one aspect at a time. Show your youngsters a picture of a typical street scene. Encourage them to suggest ways that the scene can be changed bit by bit to turn it into something far more interesting and imaginative that what it actually is. Repeat this exercise, starting with a picture that bears no resemblance to the first one.

McElligot's Pool

Published by Random House

Marco, originally of *And To Think That I Saw It On Mulberry Street*, appears again in this tall fishing tale. After reading the story aloud, ask each youngster to use assorted craft supplies to fashion a wildly imaginary fish. When the fish is complete, have him explain to his classmates where this fish's habitat is and what its distinguishing characteristics are. Display all of the fish on a bulletin board titled "Look What We Caught In McElligot's Pool."

Horton Hatches The Egg

Published by Random House

Dr. Seuss said that *Horton Hatches The Egg* was one of his favorite books. He went on to explain that although the story idea got started by accident, it was easy and enjoyable for him to write. The idea sprouted when one of his drawings of an elephant fell on his drawings of a tree. Looking at the transparent papers, he thought it was most peculiar to see an elephant in a tree. For weeks he pondered this image. Finally it clicked. The elephant was hatching an egg. And the rest of the story tumbled onto paper.

Read the story to your youngsters; then remind them that Horton was faithful—100 percent. Find out if your youngsters have ever promised to help someone, only to find that this is difficult to do. Have them discuss whether they, like Horton, were faithful to the end.

Ask youngsters to think of other animals that could have sat on the bird's egg. Ask each student to choose an animal and imagine that it was as faithful as Horton. Have each student paint a picture to show what the hatchling would look like if it was a cross between a bird and the animal that tended it. Display these creatures on a bulletin board with the title "Look What Hatched!"

Horton Hears A Who!

Published by Random House

After reading this story aloud, lead youngsters in a discussion about people in need who are often overlooked (the homeless and the elderly, for example). Then have each child cut out a bright pink clover and mount it on a bulletin board as he makes a suggestion for how to help or encourage someone in need. Choose one or more suggestions, and assist youngsters in implementing them.

Thidwick,
The Big-Hearted Moose
Published by Random House

Thidwick was another of Dr. Seuss's marvelous accidents. Seuss doodled as he chatted with a friend, Joe Warwick, on the phone. When he hung up, he realized that one of his scribbles resembled a moose with peculiar animals perched in his rack. With the seed of this thought planted in his mind, the story began to grow. An early draft of the title named the moose Warwick after the caller. But later the moose's name was changed to Thidwick.

Read this story aloud. Then have youngsters discuss times when they have noticed people wearing out their welcome. Ask them to describe times when people took advantage of the easygoing natures of others and imposed thoughtlessly. Then have student volunteers take turns playing the parts of the creatures in the story. Encourage the Thidwick character to be more assertive in trying to evict the creatures from his rack. Then have each youngster draw creatures in the moose's rack shown on page 103.

Yertle The Turtle
And Other Stories
Published by Random House

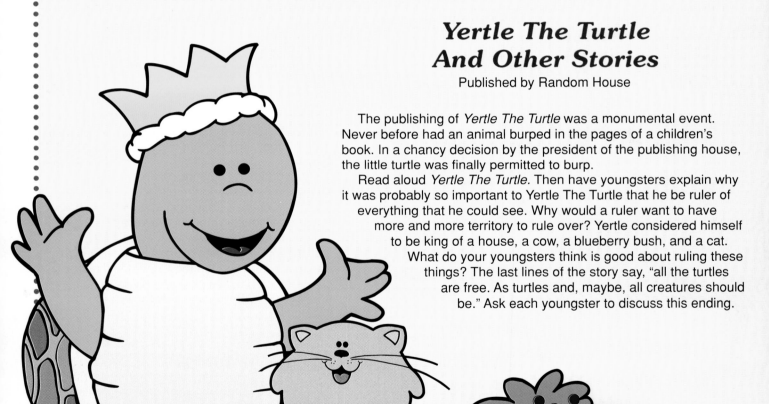

The publishing of *Yertle The Turtle* was a monumental event. Never before had an animal burped in the pages of a children's book. In a chancy decision by the president of the publishing house, the little turtle was finally permitted to burp.

Read aloud *Yertle The Turtle.* Then have youngsters explain why it was probably so important to Yertle The Turtle that he be ruler of everything that he could see. Why would a ruler want to have more and more territory to rule over? Yertle considered himself to be king of a house, a cow, a blueberry bush, and a cat. What do your youngsters think is good about ruling these things? The last lines of the story say, "all the turtles are free. As turtles and, maybe, all creatures should be." Ask each youngster to discuss this ending.

If I Ran The Zoo

Published by Random House

Theodore Geisel's dad was the superintendent of the local park system. Since Seuss's dad directed a zoo, that is probably where he came up with the idea for *If I Ran The Zoo.* Read the book aloud to your students. Then ask for volunteers to tell what their parents do for a living. Encourage each youngster to contemplate what it would be like to have the job of one of his parents. What would he do that would be different from the way his parent probably does the job?

Have students use crayons, paints, or chalk to design make-believe creatures for a McGrew's zoo. After cutting out his creature, have each child glue it to a Styrofoam meat tray. Then assist him as he places and glues strips of black construction paper on the tray to resemble a zoo cage.

Bartholomew And The Oobleck

Published by Random House

During World War II, Theodore Geisel was in France. One night the rain came down in merciless sheets. He overheard two American soldiers muttering about the weather and wishing aloud that something other than rain would fall from the sky.

Read aloud *Bartholomew And The Oobleck* to your youngsters. Ask them why the king was probably always upset with the weather. Then remind youngsters that when the kind's oobleck began to fall, disaster took over. Find out if your youngsters have ever caused problems for others. Did they opt to apologize as the king did? Discuss the magical powers of saying "I'm sorry."

Marvin K. Mooney, Will You Please Go Now!

Published by Random House

At the height of the Watergate affair, Dr. Seuss sent Art Buchwald a copy of *Marvin K. Mooney, Will You Please Go Now!* But the remarkable aspect of this gesture is that Marvin K. Mooney's name had been replaced with the name Richard M. Nixon. Knowing this, you'll never glean the same meaning from this book again!

The ouster in this book wanted Marvin K. Mooney to leave by any means imaginable—just as long as he went. Have each youngster think of a silly, creative way to travel. Then have him draw a picture that shows Marvin leaving by that means. As each youngster dictates, write a completion for "You can go on (by)…." Bind these drawings into a book titled "Please Go Now!"

The Cat In The Hat

Published by Random House

In 1957, Dr. Seuss published a book like no other that had preceded it. Using only 220 words, he turned the children's book market on its ear. The zippy rhymes and outlandish plot of *The Cat In The Hat,* paired with its easy readability, propelled Dr. Seuss to fame.

After reading this story aloud, produce a large red box. Explain that the Cat in the Hat left the box, saying that Thing One and Thing Two aren't in there. But some really weird creatures are. Have each youngster use a variety of supplies to fashion a creature for the Cat's box. When the creatures are done, place them in the box. Take one creature at a time from the box, and have its creator introduce it and tell about it and any trouble it is likely to cause.

Oh, The Places You'll Go!
Published by Random House

Dr. Seuss's last book, *Oh, The Places You'll Go!*, was published one year before his death. It remained on the *New York Times* best-seller list for over two years. Its pages overflow with wisdom and positivism.

Read aloud *Oh, The Places You'll Go!* to your youngsters. Then have each student find a picture of some place he'd like to go and attach it to a display along with a picture that shows something he'd like to do. When each student has contributed to the display, have him tell his classmates about the things he hopes to do and the places he'd like to go.

The Lorax
Published by Random House

It seems Dr. Seuss was an environmentalist all along. *The Lorax* was his personal favorite of his writings. Read the story to your youngsters or show the video or film. Then ask your youngsters if they are aware of any animals or plants that are going the way of the truffula trees. Have them propose ways that they can help protect the environment. Post a list of these suggestions on a board with the title "Listen To The Lorax."

Happy Birthday To You!
Published by Random House

Theodore Geisel was born on March 2, 1904. Celebrate his birthday by reading aloud *Happy Birthday To You!* Throw a big party for the occasion. Invite other classes to attend, and allow youngsters to view Dr. Seuss films or videos as they share a snack—perhaps green eggs and ham.

Crazy About Shel Silverstein

In *The New Read-Aloud Handbook*, Jim Trelease says Shel Silverstein's books *A Light In The Attic* and *Where The Sidewalk Ends* are the most frequently stolen library books. That's quite a compliment—in an unusual sort of way. Other distinctions of *Where The Sidewalk Ends* include the fact that it was on the *New York Times* adult best-seller list for more than 80 weeks, has sales that actually increased rather than decreased with time, and has two million copies in print.

Who is the man behind the magical poetry? Before his death in 1999, Silverstein was a dynamo who had a long-standing relationship with *Playboy* as a cartoonist. But he also wrote many hit songs, most of them country. His biggest hit, "A Boy Named Sue," was recorded in the 1960s by Johnny Cash at Folsom Prison. "The Unicorn," a hit for The Irish Rovers; "One's On The Way" performed by Loretta Lynn; and "Cover Of The Rolling Stone" performed by Dr. Hook And The Medicine Show are a smattering of other songs that Shel Silverstein wrote. But poetry, cartooning, and writing music were not the limits of his talents. He was also a playwright.

Approaching adolescence, Silverstein would have preferred to be an athlete or a ladies' man. But since he was neither, he turned to drawing and writing. *Something About The Author* quoted interview-shy Silverstein as saying, "You can go crazy with some of the wonderful stuff there is in life." Thanks to Shel Silverstein's wonderful writing, there's a lot more wonderful stuff to be crazy about!

Use the following ideas with the works of Shel Silverstein to create some magical, meaningful learning opportunities.

"Backward Bill"

Read "Backward Bill" from *A Light In The Attic.* Then have a backward day of your own. Notify parents in advance that your class will be having backward day. Ask that children wear at least one clothing item backward on the designated day. Meanwhile make your lesson plans in reverse order, starting with the last thing you usually do during the day and progressing toward your first hello. When backward day arrives call on students using their surnames first, then their given names. During lunch eat the dessert first, then the rest of the meal. Throughout the day, add your own personal backward touches, as well as those that students recommend. And—by all means—have N-U-F!

Michelle Therrien—Pre/K
Bright Horizons Children's Center
Cheshire, MA

"Rock N' Roll Band"

After reading "Rock N' Roll Band" from *A Light In The Attic,* discuss different types of musical instruments. Have students help you make a graph of different types of instruments found in a music catalog. Also have students listen to a recording of instruments, and identify the instrument from which the sound came. Encourage students to find items around the classroom to use as makeshift instruments. Reread the poem and have students parade around your classroom "playing" their unusual instruments.

Lois Waltz—Pre/K
Corpus Christi School
Howell, NJ

"Crowded Tub"

This suggestion for using "Crowded Tub" from Shel Silverstein's *A Light In The Attic* is bubbling over with zany fun. Read the poem to your youngsters, and show them the illustration. Then give each youngster a paper plate and access to a variety of art supplies and scraps. Have each student decorate the plate to resemble his face. Then mount the paper-plate portraits above a tub cutout bearing the poem. Student-made arm and leg cutouts may be added too. Have students cut various sizes of paper circles and attach them to the bulletin board for the bubbles floating up from and spilling out of the tub.

Angelina Argonza—Preschool
Rainbow Bridge Preschool
San Jose, CA

"Thumb Face"

From *A Light In The Attic,* read aloud "Thumb Face." Provide each student with drawing paper and crayons. Assist each child in outlining a giant thumb shape. Then reread the poem, pausing after each description of the thumb's appearance so that each student may draw and color his thumb accordingly. Have students share and discuss their drawings with their classmates. No doubt each thumb face will have its own character, and each will be quite different!

Lorie Cook—Gr. K
Dr. Charles T. Lunsford School #19
Rochester, NY

"I'm Making A List"

Use Shel Silverstein's poem "I'm Making A List" from *Where The Sidewalk Ends* to stimulate discussions about courtesy and to exercise students' sight-word skills. To prepare for this activity, write each of the eight courteous expressions from the poem on a different color of card. Then program three sets of oversize color-coded cards to match and attach them randomly to your classroom floor. Read the poem; then ask students to interpret the poem. Talk about the fact that the phrase "stick them in your eye" is an expression not to be taken literally, but to express disdain. Briefly discuss other expressions (such as "Take a hike," and "Oh, go fly a kite.") that are not to be taken literally. Then ask why the author, who seemed to be encouraging such good manners, would end the poem on such a note. Help students see the human and comical side in this change of tune.

Talk about the polite words Mr. Silverstein included in this poem. Hold up your small deck of cards and read through the courteous expressions with your students. Then have students examine the matching expression cards on the floor. To begin play, hold up a card and read the expression as students find a matching card on the floor and stand with their feet by (but not covering) it. More than one student may stand by a single card. Continue play by holding and reading additional cards and having students stand by corresponding floor cards.

Karen Jendro—Preschool
Pumpkin Patch Preschool
Monticello, MN

"What's In The Sack?"

Read aloud "What's In The Sack?" from *Where The Sidewalk Ends*. Then ask students to speculate about what might be in this enormous sack. Ask each child to draw, color, and cut out what he thinks the contents are. Then have him glue the drawing to a sheet of construction paper. On top of the drawing, have him glue a cutout of a sack so that it can be lifted up to reveal the picture beneath. As he dictates, write the child's comments about the sack's contents on the construction paper. Punch holes in the margin of each student's page and compile the pages in a booklet that has a copy of the poem "What's In The Sack?" on its first page.

Stephanie Santos—Gr. K/1, St. Andrew School,
Waynesboro, PA

"Hector The Collector"

Read aloud "Hector The Collector" from *Where The Sidewalk Ends*. Ask the children to recall things that Hector collected, which might initially appear to be junk. As they do, list the items that they name on the board. Have each child propose a way to reuse one item from the list. Encourage youngsters to draw pictures showing how they would reuse the items. Or provide some of the things mentioned in the poem and have students turn them into exciting things with the help of a parent or older student.

Stephanie Santos—Gr. K/1

"The Toucan"

Read aloud "The Toucan" from *Where The Sidewalk Ends.* Have students brainstorm ideas for additional verses. As they dictate, record their additional verses or send a note to parents asking that they assist their youngsters in writing additional verses for the poem. Then have the students work together to paint, color, or otherwise colorize an oversize outline of a toucan. Display the finished toucan as the focal point of a bulletin board bearing the original poem and also the students' additions.

Stephanie Santos—Gr. K/1
St. Andrew School
Waynesboro, PA

"Invisible Boy"

If you're going to use this suggestion, mime or acting skills will come in handy. Show students a large sheet of blank paper clipped to an easel and a chart tablet onto which "Invisible Boy" from *Where The Sidewalk Ends* has been copied. Make a fuss over the artwork that appears above the poem, pointing out the detail and humor in the drawings of the imaginary boy, house, cheese, and mouse. Reread Silverstein's challenge in the last line of the poem: "Will you draw an invisible picture for me?" Using a portion of a sentence strip, cover each of the words at the ends of the first four lines of the copied poem. With the assistance of your youngsters, choose a replacement word to write on each sentence strip. Read the revised poem to your youngsters. Then delight them by setting out invisible crayons and painstakingly "drawing" an imaginary pic-ture. When you're done, stand back, admire your work, and ask your students to critique it.

Invite student volunteers (one at a time) to supply new words for the ends of the first four lines of the poem. Then have them "draw" and admire their works. If desired, provide each student with a copy of the poem minus the last word in each of the first four lines, and help them fill in the blanks before displaying their amazing in-visible projects.

Rona E. Forman—Gr. K, P.S. 236-Mill Basin School, Brooklyn, NY

"The Yipiyuk"

"The Yipiyuk" is a wonderfully imaginative poem from *Where The Sidewalk Ends.* The poem is about a fictitious creature that attaches itself to a man's foot and refuses to let go, so the man hobbles throughout his life with a Yipiyuk stuck to his toe. To begin this activity, write the word *Yipiyuk* on the board and have the class brainstorm ideas of what a Yipiyuk could be. Then, without showing the picture, read the poem to the class. Have the students close their eyes and visualize the creature called a Yipiyuk. Divide your students into small groups and have each group answer these pertinent questions about the Yipiyuk: What does it look like?, Where does it live?, What does it eat?, What does it drink?, What does it do for fun? After each group arrives at a complete description of a Yipiyuk and its lifestyle, have each group report on its answers to the questions. Record the responses of each group; then have students compare the results.

To close the activity, play "The Yipiyuk" from Shel Silverstein's recording of *Where The Sidewalk Ends;* then show students the poet's illustration of the Yipiyuk and discuss their reactions.

Kimberly Amsden—Gr. K
Lake Grove Elementary
Federal Way, WA

"Hug O' War"

Reading Shel Silverstein's poem "Hug O' War" from *Where The Sidewalk Ends* is an excellent way to introduce a cooperative theme. When you see that students are having difficulty dealing with feelings of competition, ask the group to sit in a circle and listen to a reading of "Hug O' War." Talk with your youngsters about cooperation. Then play a recording of music and ask each student to attempt to give each of his classmates a hug before the music is done. Ask students to come back into a circle; then discuss how much nicer it is when everyone wins.

Suzanne Costner—Preschool
Holy Trinity Pre-Kindergarten
Fayetteville, NC

HUG O' WAR

I will not play at tug o' war.
I'd rather play at hug o' war,
Where everyone hugs
Instead of tugs,
Where everyone giggles
And rolls on the rug,
Where everyone kisses,
And everyone grins,
And everyone cuddles,
And everyone wins.

Giving To The Tree

After reading *The Giving Tree,* have the children reverse the story and make a book titled "The Giving Children." For this book, have each child draw a picture showing something she would do for a tree. As she dictates, write her description of this gesture near her picture. You'll be amazed by the creative and caring ideas the children will imagine. Compile the pictures and bind them into a book to be enjoyed at the book corner.

Michelle Therrien—Pre/K
Bright Horizons Children's Center
Cheshire, MA

Trees Of Their Own

If your lesson plans include reading aloud and discussing *The Giving Tree,* consider this suggestion for unique impact. After you've read the story aloud, present each youngster with his own sapling. Encourage youngsters to plant and tend their trees and to update their classmates on the growth or changes in their saplings. This is a good way to foster responsibility and to encourage scientific observation skills.

Sherri Brayfield—Pre/K, Marietta First Baptist Wee Center Acworth, GA

The Missing Piece

Watch your students' eyes sparkle with delight as you present the story *The Missing Piece.* You will need to prepare some simple props in advance. Start by cutting a wedge from a Styrofoam® circle. The wedge will be the missing piece. Insert a dowel in the back of the Styrofoam® circle so that you can roll it much like the circle in the story rolls. Cut other Styrofoam® pieces (one that is too small, one that is too big, one that's too square, etc.) to match the elements in the story. Also collect an imitation flower, butterfly, and bug. Before telling the story, teach your class the song that the missing piece sings. Then tell the story of *The Missing Piece* as you use the props to enact it, having children join in on the song.

Lori Schumaker—Jr. K, Sacred Heart School, Grand Rapids, MI

More Of Shel Silverstein

Recordings
Where The Sidewalk Ends Cassette
A Light In The Attic Cassette

Books
The Missing Piece Meets The Big O
A Giraffe And A Half
Lafcadio:The Lion Who Shot Back
Who Wants A Cheap Rhinoceros?

In Step With Steig

The timeless quality and witty illustrations of William Steig's stories render him the incomparable master of the contemporary picture book. Woven with charm and fantasy, Steig's tales captivate youngsters and adults alike. Choose from among the following classroom-tested ideas to keep your balanced-reading program in step with Steig.

William Steig was born on November 14, 1907, into an artistic family. He began a successful career as a cartoonist in 1930. However, it was not until 1968 that he published his first children's book, *Roland The Minstrel Pig.* Steig once said that each of his children's books, with the exception of one, began as a visual image without a theme: "…I just ramble around and discover for myself what will happen next." Steig has been the recipient of numerous awards including Caldecott Medals in 1970 for *Sylvester And The Magic Pebble* and in 1977 for *The Amazing Bone.*

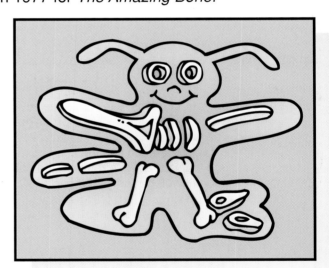

Amazing Pretzel Bones

After reading *The Amazing Bone,* have youngsters help you follow the recipe to make these tasty treats. Dissolve yeast in warm water. Stir in sugar and salt. Gradually mix in flour. Turn dough out onto a floured surface and knead until it's elastic. Have each youngster mold a small amount of dough into a bone shape and place it on a cookie sheet. Brush the top of each youngster's bone with beaten egg; then have him sprinkle it with salt. Bake the bones for 12–15 minutes in a 425° oven. No bones about it, these treats are delicious!

Deanna P. Groke—Child Development
Medical Lake, WA

Boning Up

Boning up on classification skills is a great way to follow up the reading of *The Amazing Bone.* Have youngsters bring clean meat bones to school. When the collection is complete, have youngsters classify the bones by size, type, and texture. Then have youngsters glue the bones atop a length of bulletin-board paper to resemble a skeleton. Challenge them to draw around the bones to reveal the creature to whom the bones might belong. Have youngsters name their creature, then dictate a related story as you write it on chart paper. It's a "Bone-na-fide" hit!

Mary Beth Heath, Murrells Inlet, SC

Amazing Pretzel Bones

2 tsp. dry yeast
1¹/₂ cups warm water
1 Tbs. sugar
1 tsp. salt
4 cups flour
beaten egg
salt

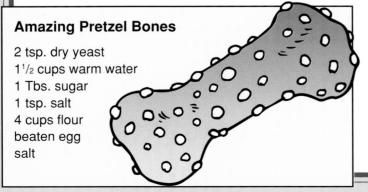

Solomon The Rusty Nail

Solomon was a prize pazoozle of a rabbit—if he scratched his nose and wiggled his toes at exactly the same time, he could become a rusty nail. Chances are, your classroom is filled with prize pazoozles of youngsters, each with his own unique talent! To recognize youngsters' talents, place slips of paper bearing youngsters' names in a container. Have each youngster draw out a classmate's name, then dictate as you complete a corresponding award. Have each youngster add an illustration to the award; then present it to the honoree at an awards ceremony.

Pam Warren—Gr. K
DeSoto Trail School
Tallahassee, FL

The Zabajaba Jungle

Zabajaba Nectar is perfect for sipping during the reading of *The Zabajaba Jungle.* In a large bowl, have youngsters stir together one quart of softened, vanilla ice cream and one quart of softened orange sherbet. Then have them gradually stir in one quart of orange juice and one quart of ginger ale. Spoon the nectar into cups and serve with straws. "Zabajaba-licious!"

Deanna P. Groke—Pre/K
Medical Lake, WA

Amos & Boris

Sometimes different is better, and your youngsters are sure to agree after they hear *Amos & Boris.* As a follow-up activity, have youngsters brainstorm a list of the similarities and differences between mice and whales as you write them on a chart. But how are a mouse and an elephant alike? Why, they can both be gray!

Jan Ross—Media Specialist
Dixie Elementary Magnet School
Lexington, KY

Brave Irene

Mrs. Bobbin's creation for the duchess will pale in comparison to your youngsters' original designs! After reading *Brave Irene* aloud, have youngsters design original dresses for the duchess. Have each youngster glue a fabric dress cutout to a sheet of construction paper, then trim away the excess paper. Then have each youngster glue lace, ribbon, sequins, buttons, and other festive trimmings atop his cutout. On a bulletin board, mount a colored cutout resembling Irene, a dress box, and a large tree cutout. Display youngsters' completed creations on the tree. Won't the duchess be delighted!

Dawn Hurley, Bethel Park, PA

Sylvester And The Magic Pebble

What Luck!

Lucky Sylvester found a magic pebble! Chances are your youngsters have had similar strokes of luck that they would enjoy sharing. Have each youngster dictate as you type (on a computer) his completion to this story starter: "The luckiest day of my life was…." Have the youngster select computer graphics to illustrate his story, then print out a copy. Mount the illustrated stories on a bulletin board along with a donkey cutout and the title "Strokes Of Luck!"

Barbara Moffatt
George's Creek School
Lonaconing, MD

Magic Pebble News

Two Sad Parents

A Missing Donkey

Pebble Pals

Rock your classroom with pebble pals! After reading *Sylvester And The Magic Pebble* aloud, take your youngsters outside on pebble patrol. Have each youngster search the school grounds for the perfect pebble, then bring his prized pebble back inside and share it with his classmates. To create pebble pals, have youngsters use assorted arts-and-crafts materials to decorate their pebbles. Move over, Pet Rocks; pebble pals are here to stay!

Keetette Turner—Gr. K
Woodstock School
Sandy, UT

The Luckiest Day Of My Life

The luckiest day of my life was the day I found a four-leaf clover. I took it home. I didn't know it was lucky. I found out it was lucky when I made a wish. I wished for a clown to bring me balloons, and he did!

by Cheri

A Nose For News

Sylvester's strange disappearance and amazing return are certainly newsworthy events! So why not let your little reporters give the scoop on Sylvester by writing their own newspaper articles? Explain to youngsters that every newspaper article must tell *who, what, where, when,* and *how.* Then have youngsters take turns dictating sentences for Sylvester-related articles as you write them on chart paper. Later type the articles using a newspaper format, being sure to leave space for accompanying "photos." Duplicate student copies; then have each youngster illustrate his copy. Extra! Extra! Read all about it!

Lorna Vander Sluis—Gr. K
Calvin Christian School
Wyoming, MI

Sylvester's Seasons

Sylvester's existence as a rock spans an entire year and provides little ones with a perfect review of the seasons. After reading the story aloud, label each of four areas of your classroom with the name of or symbol for a different season. For a cooperative-learning activity, have a different group of youngsters assemble in each of the four areas and discuss the characteristics of its season. Then have each group design a poster or mural to represent its season. To culminate the activity, ask each group member to share something about his group's poster with his classmates.

Diane Warrick—Gr. K
Evergreen Elementary
Midlothian, VA

Rebus Collectibles

Sylvester was quite the collector! He found the magic pebble while searching for pebbles to add to his collection. Invite each youngster to bring a sample of his own collectibles to school. Have youngsters display their collections and tell their classmates about them. Program a sentence strip, similar to the ones shown, for each youngster. Have each youngster write his name on his strip, then glue on a few items from his collection or attach stickers or illustrations that represent his collection. If desired, program a strip for Sylvester, too. Display the completed strips end-to-end for a collectible rebus.

Jacqueline Vitek—Gr. K
Ben Franklin Kindergarten Center
Dupont, PA

Mike collects .

Alicia collects .

Pebble Pendants

Polish youngsters' storytelling skills with pebble pendants. In advance, duplicate student copies of a booklet page similar to the one shown. Have each youngster thread a magic pebble (red bead) onto a length of yarn. Tie the ends of each youngster's yarn length around his neck to create a pendant. Then, while touching his magic pebble, have each youngster make a wish. Next have him write his name in the appropriate spaces on his booklet page, then write or dictate a completion for the sentence. Have each youngster add a corresponding illustration. Bind the completed pages between construction-paper covers; then label the front cover as desired. Youngsters can wear their pendants home and retell Sylvester's story to their families.

Joan Daly—Gr. K
Lordship School
Stratford, CT

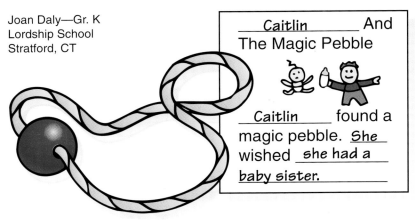

    Caitlin   And
The Magic Peble

    Caitlin   found a
magic pebble. She
wished she had a
baby sister.

Wishes

This cooperative project is long on wishes! After discussing Sylvester's wish with youngsters, spread out a length of bulletin-board paper on the floor. Position youngsters along one side of the paper, designating an area for each one. Give each youngster a "magic" pebble. Ask each youngster to close his eyes and make a wish; then allow volunteers to share their wishes with their classmates. Have each youngster illustrate his wish on his portion of the paper; then have him dictate a sentence about his wish as you write it below his illustration. Mount the completed project in the hall for passersby to enjoy. Wishes really do come true!

adapted from an idea by
Susan Davis Miller—Gr. K
Bethesda Elementary
Lawrenceville, GA

Good Wishes, Bad Wishes

Sylvester's wish to become a rock saved him from a lion but caused problems that he had never imagined! After reading *Sylvester And The Magic Pebble* aloud, have youngsters pass around a small pebble that has been painted red. As each youngster holds the pebble, have him share a wish with his classmates. Allow youngsters to predict what the consequences of their wishes might be. Then, for even more wishful thinking, share *Three Wishes* written by M. Jean Craig and illustrated by Yuri Salzman (1986, Scholastic Inc.).

Trudy Hines
East Canyon Elementary
Caldwell, ID

Pebble Painting

Rock and roll with pebble painting! For each youngster, add a small amount of red tempera paint to a paper cup. Have each youngster place one pebble in his cup, then roll the pebble around to coat it with paint. Then have each youngster slip a piece of paper inside a Ziploc® bag, add his coated pebble, seal the bag, and shake it to create a pebble painting. While youngsters are shaking their bags, add a small amount of glue to each youngster's cup. Then help youngsters remove their paintings and set them aside to dry. Have each youngster remove the pebble from his bag, place it in his cup, and roll it around to coat it with the paint-and-glue mixture. Youngsters then remove their coated pebbles, place them atop sheets of newspaper, and sprinkle them with red glitter. What dazzling magic pebbles!

Jennifer Strathdee—Pre/K Special Education
Parkside School
Auburn, NY

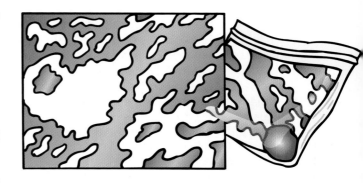

A Touch Of Class

A magic pebble adds a touch of class to this special booklet. In advance, duplicate student copies of a blank booklet page similar to the one shown. Use an X-acto® knife to cut out the circle in the bottom right-hand side of each copy. For inspiration, provide each youngster with a pebble that has been painted with red tempera. Have each youngster rub his magic pebble, think of a wish, then illustrate his wish on his copy of the booklet page. Complete each youngster's copy as he dictates. Cut two poster-board booklet covers, slightly larger than the booklet pages. Place a booklet page atop each cover; then trace the cut-out circle onto each cover. For a back cover, glue a "magic pebble" inside the circle. For a front cover, cut out the traced circle with an X-acto® knife and decorate it as desired. Stack each youngster's completed page atop the back cover, position the front cover in place, and staple the booklet together. This tactile sensation will rock your classroom library!

Terry Muth—Gr. K
Salem Heights School
Salem, OR

Edible Pebbles

Try this sweet follow-up to *Sylvester And The Magic Pebble*. In a box, place a supply of wrapped, red, "pebblelike" candy. After reading the story aloud, pass around the box and allow each youngster to select a piece of candy. Next have each youngster rub his candy and make a wish. After youngsters have had an opportunity to share their wishes with their classmates, allow them to unwrap their treats and pop them into their mouths.

Cindy Schumacher
Prairie Elementary School
Cottonwood, ID

Doctor De Soto

Smiles For Doctor De Soto

Put smiles on youngsters' faces with this estimation activity. Cut a supply of red construction-paper mouths. Have each youngster glue a mouth cutout atop a sheet of construction paper. Then have him estimate the number of teeth (navy beans) that would fit inside the mouth. Have each youngster glue navy beans inside his cutout to resemble teeth, then count the number of beans he used. Have each youngster compare his estimate to the actual number of beans he used. Display the completed mouths on a bulletin board with a colored character resembling Dr. De Soto. What beautiful pearly whites!

Karin McKeen—Gr. K
Searsport Elementary
Searsport, ME

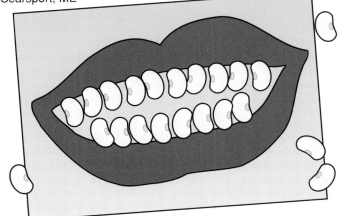

Doctor De Soto's Office

As a follow-up to *Doctor De Soto,* youngsters will enjoy pretending to be dentists and dental assistants through dramatic play. Designate an area in your classroom to be Doctor De Soto's office. Include a reception area complete with a telephone, sign-in sheet, and magazines, and an examining room with a mock dental chair. While working, have the dentist and dental assistant don old, white shirts and surgical masks. The dental assistant calls a stuffed-animal patient from the reception area, then preps him for the dentist. Using tongue depressors, rubber gloves, and other dental tools, the dentist and dental assistant perform dental procedures on the stuffed animal. Open, please.

Stacy Leonard—Pre/K
North Elementary
Lamesa, TX

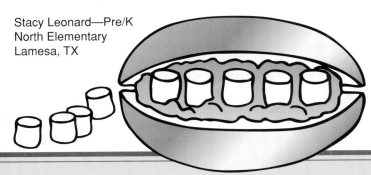

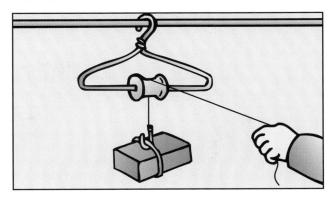

Pulley Power

Put some of Doctor DeSoto's pulley power to work in your block center. Set up several simple pulleys in your block center. Allow youngsters to experiment by lifting different-sized loads with the pulleys. It's easy to lighten a load with a little pulley power.

Michelle Sears—Preschool
Malone Head Start
Queensbury, NY

Chair, Ladder, Pulley

Size up potential patients for Doctor De Soto with this follow-up activity. Place a set of animal pictures or cards in a paper bag. Display a different card with each of the following illustrations: Doctor De Soto standing beside his dental chair, Doctor De Soto on his ladder, and Doctor De Soto hanging from his pulley. Have youngsters discuss the three methods that Doctor De Soto used to examine his patients. Then have each youngster draw a picture from the bag and specify which of the three examination methods Doctor De Soto might use if the animal were his patient. Have youngsters give reasons for their choices, then identify any special problems that each patient might create.

Stacy Leonard—Pre/K

Lip Smackers

Your Doctor De Soto fans will delight in making these lip-smackin' treats! To make a treat, spread peanut butter between two apple wedges; then press the wedges together to resemble a mouth. Press miniature-marshmallow "teeth" into the peanut butter. These nutritious treats will be a hit with your youngsters *and* their dentists!

Fran C. Nelson
West Lenoir Elementary
Lenoir, NC

Tales...By Tafuri

Using Nancy Tafuri's Books In Your Classroom

Being an only child until she was ten years old, Nancy Tafuri learned to enjoy her own company by coloring and painting for hours at a time! This love of art followed her into young adulthood when she entered the School of Visual Arts in New York City. "I adored shapes—" says the grown-up Nancy, "big, round, inviting shapes...which I felt would be perfect for the very young." And she was right! Children of all ages love her simple, uncluttered, yet emotionally affecting work. Nancy says that one of life's joys for her is "being able to take short lines of text or, in most cases, none at all and turn them into a package that can be held by small hands." So unwrap a package or two that was created with care—especially for your little ones—by Nancy Tafuri.

Have You Seen My Duckling?
Published by Greenwillow Books

Oh, no—a duckling is missing! Mother Duck and the rest of her brood swim around the pond frantically searching for the missing duckling. Page by page, clever viewers will soon realize that the little duckling really isn't lost at all— just adventuring. After sharing this book with your youngsters, create lots of opportunities for creative writing and sequencing events. Start by mounting a large construction-paper pond on a bulletin board. Then have each child use art materials to make a different character from the story— including the nest. (If you have more students than characters in the book, have some children embellish the pond scene with construction-paper details.) Then read the story again. As each character appears in the story, have a child pin the corresponding character to the board. Encourage children to improvise dialogue for each of the "speechless" characters in the story. Write the dialogue on paper speech bubbles; then mount the bubbles on the board. Add a title and you've got a wonderful display that youngsters can use to tell the story again and again!

Donna Adkins—Gr. K, Perritt Primary, Arkadelphia, AR

Early Morning In The Barn
Published by Greenwillow Books

When the sun comes up, the chicks are off to say "Good morning" to each of the barn's residents. The result? Well, try it in your classroom and see for yourself! As each new sound word is introduced in this book, assign the sound to a child or small group of children. Encourage each child to study her word and remember what it looks like. Then each time you point to that particular word, she can voice the part. Soon you'll have an original barnyard symphony in your classroom! Read the book again, switching parts as desired.

After sharing in a participatory reading of Early Morning In The Barn (see above), youngsters will be primed for this story-related reading activity. For each character in the book, cut out a tagboard card. Draw a picture of each animal in the book. Cut out each picture; then glue each picture to the left side of a different tagboard card. Write each animal's corresponding sound word on the right side of the card. Then make a puzzle cut between each picture and word. Store all of the pieces in a string-tie envelope. To do this activity, encourage children to use their reading skills to match each word to an animal picture.

Donna Adkins—Gr. K

Dig a little further into the farm theme by encouraging students to create a classroom farm in your block area or sand table. Use toy animals, buildings, and people from your classroom collection. If you're short on any items, encourage children to create them using craft supplies. Keep a copy of the book close by so that youngsters can act out the story with their own farm.

Nancy Clements—Pre-K and K, The Children's Center New York, NY

Who's Counting?
Published by Greenwillow Books

Who's counting? For starters, one curious little puppy! Youngsters can count along as this little puppy pads across the fields and through the barnyard to his final destination. After sharing this book with your students, have each child make a counting book of his own. First give each child ten sheets of paper. Instruct each child to write a different numeral and/or number word from one to ten on each page. Then have each child draw pictures to correspond with the number on each page. (Use rubber stamps for variety.) Bind each child's pages between construction-paper covers; then have him color and title the cover. Encourage each child to share his book during a group reading time.

Adapted from an idea by Samita Arora
Rainbows United, Inc., Wichita, KS

This counting book will be one of your students' favorite reading projects. Choose the numbers that you would like to study (for example, one–ten). For each number, position a child near a given number of objects (such as one hamster, two dress-up hats, etc); then snap a picture. Also take a picture of your entire class. For the last number, take a picture of that many children running; then take another picture of the same number of children playing. Program a sheet of construction paper for each number that you have included in your pictures. On the next-to-last page, write "[Ten] children…" On the last page, write "playing!" Glue the pictures to the corresponding pages and bind them all between two covers. Glue the class picture to the cover. You might even want to laminate this best-seller!

Mary Sutula, Orlando, FL

Ten children... playing!

Rabbit's Morning
Published by Greenwillow Books

When the sun was hot, Rabbit began his journey home. Nancy Tafuri invites the viewer to travel alongside Rabbit. Use this story as a springboard to discussing ordinal numbers and sequence of events. In advance, photocopy each of the animals in the book. (Be sure to include the mouse, hummingbird, opossum, swan, beaver, frog, porcupine, deer, pheasant, raccoon, skunk, and ladybug.) Mount each picture on construction paper. Next, leaving space between each word, write the ordinal number words (first–twelfth) across the board. Then share the story with your children. Afterwards ask children to recall which characters Rabbit saw first, second, third, etc. Mount the characters on the board under the appropriate ordinal number word. (Use the book as a research tool to recall the sequence of events.) Some of the order of events will be left up to class discretion!

Adapted from an idea by
Sharon Roop—Gr. K
Slate Hill Elementary
Worthington, OH

What has a fin?

A shark has a fin!

Spots, Feathers, And Curly Tails
Published by Greenwillow Books

What causes youngsters' imaginations to kick into gear? Nancy Tafuri's Spots, Feathers, And Curly Tails! Before reading, show youngsters the cover of this book. Ask them to think about the title and the illustration to determine the setting of this book. When they have determined that it takes place on a farm, read the book aloud. Encourage youngsters to guess the answers to the text's questions before you turn the pages. Then choose another setting (such as the ocean or the zoo) and have each child think of an appropriate animal. Next give each child a large sheet of construction paper to fold in half. Instruct him to write a question about his animal on the folded side of the paper and illustrate it. Then have him open the paper and draw the entire animal on the inside. Have each child refold his paper and have the class try to guess his animal.

More Books By Nancy Tafuri
(Greenwillow Books)

The Barn Party
Do Not Disturb
Follow Me!
Junglewalk
This Is The Farmer

Books Illustrated By Nancy Tafuri

Flap Your Wings And Try • Written by Charlotte Pomerantz

Asleep, Asleep • Written by Mirra Ginsburg

Across The Stream • Written by Mirra Ginsburg

WELCOME TO WADDELL'S WORLD

Adventure, fun, and—most especially—emotion are the key elements in the worlds created by Martin Waddell. Although fictitious in nature, Waddell's works are inspired by the real experiences and emotions of children—separation anxiety, fear of the dark, the desire for friendship, and the joy of childhood fun. Use some of these activities with Martin Waddell's stories; then promote parent-child reading experiences by sending each child home with a copy of the bookmark on page 120. (All books mentioned are published by Candlewick Press unless otherwise noted.)

by Mackie Rhodes

CAN'T YOU SLEEP, LITTLE BEAR?
Illustrated by Barbara Firth

Little Bear's fear of the dark persists until Big Bear's loving gesture alleviates Little Bear's fear, making room for sleep. After sharing the story, explore Little Bear's fear with youngsters. Then take a turn into science by inviting students to explore the amount of light needed to expel the dark. To prepare, cut out two black construction-paper circles sized to cover a large flashlight lens. Cut a circle from the middle of each lens cover—one small and the other a bit larger. Tape the first lens cover to the flashlight. Place a masking-tape line on the floor near a sheet of black bulletin-board paper attached to a wall. Dim the lights; then have a child stand on the line and shine the flashlight onto the paper. Ask another child to use chalk to trace the ring of light onto the paper. Then replace the first lens cover with the second cover and repeat the process, helping the child center the light over the first ring. Repeat the process once more, using no lens cover. Then have youngsters compare the light-ring sizes. How much dark was expelled by the light with and without the lens covers? Which lighting situation do students think would be most comfortable for Little Bear? For themselves? The resulting discoveries will be "en-light-ening!"

I hear a woofer.

LET'S GO HOME, LITTLE BEAR
Illustrated by Barbara Firth

A carefree romp through the woods takes a fearful turn as Little Bear tunes in to the noises all around. After sharing this story, challenge youngsters to sharpen their listening skills by tuning in to the noises all around them. Ask students to stop their movements, then to listen and look—just as Little Bear did in the story. After a brief time, invite each child, in turn, to describe a noise he heard during the silence—such as *"woof, woof, woof."* Then encourage each child to illustrate and label the real or imaginary source of that sound. Compile the illustrations into a class book titled "Sounds All Around." Share the book with the class, inviting each child to tell about his page.

SAILOR BEAR
Illustrated by Virginia Austin

Lost and lonely, Small Bear unintentionally reasons himself into a dangerous adventure with a most surprising conclusion. Read the story aloud; then present each child with a situation that will prompt her to adopt Small Bear's self-inquiry, "Now what shall I do?" and his problem-solving skills. To prepare, gather a group of related and unrelated items—such as a sheet of paper, a crayon, a shoe, a block, scissors, and tape—and put them into a basket. Ask a child to think about how she might combine and use some of the items from the basket; then invite her to demonstrate her idea. For example, she might use the crayon to trace the shoe onto the paper, then cut out the shoe outline and tape it onto a wall. If desired, vary the items in the basket for each student. Now what shall *I* do? Gather, group, and get youngsters thinking!

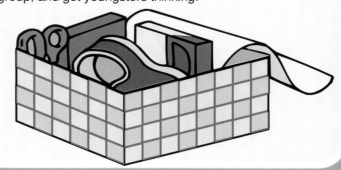

OWL BABIES
Illustrated by Patrick Benson

When they awaken to discover their mother missing, Sarah, Percy, and Bill—the young owl siblings—anxiously speculate over her whereabouts, her doings, and her safe return. After sharing the story, liken the anxiety of the young owls to that your students might have during a separation from their parents. With warm acceptance of their feelings, guide youngsters to express and explore the emotions they experience when their parents are not present. Conclude the discussion by reassuring students that their feelings and fears are understandable and acceptable. Then ask each child to imagine that Owl Mother is his parent. Where would *she* have gone? Invite the child to illustrate his conclusion, then write (or dictate) a statement about his illustration. Display the pictures with the title "My Owl Mother Went…"

Mother Owl went to buy food.

THE HAPPY HEDGEHOG BAND
Illustrated by Jill Barton

Tum-tum-te-tum. Buzz. Click. Hum. Dickon Woods jams to the beat of Harry's drum. Infect your class with the rhythmic lines in this upbeat tale about a noise-crazy hedgehog; then invite youngsters to form a rhythm band of their own. Have each child select a rhythm instrument or choose a sound that he can make—such as clapping, humming, tongue clicking, or lip smacking. Beat a few rounds of a simple rhythm on a drum; then have the class band imitate that rhythm until you raise your drumsticks to stop the music. Begin a new rhythm with a different beat or tempo. Better clear lots of space for this activity—once youngsters get the rhythm of the beat, they're bound to get the rhythm in their feet!

SQUEAK-A-LOT
Illustrated by Virginia Miller
Published by Greenwillow Books
(This book is out of print. Check your library.)

While searching for a playmate, a small mouse learns that there are some games he enjoys a lot—and some he prefers not! Read this delightfully repetitious book aloud; then transfer the story's word theme to a modified game of tag. Outdoors, have students role-play mice gathered in a designated safe zone. Appoint one child to be the cat and to remain outside the safe zone. To play, the cat calls out an action word with *a-lot* attached to it—such as *hop-a-lot.* The mice perform that action, scattering around the play area outside the safe zone until the cat calls out "Wham! Bam! Scram!" At that time, the mice scurry back to the safe zone as the cat tries to tag them. The cat then chooses his replacement from the untagged mice in the safe zone. This is one game youngsters are sure to like a lot!

MORE WONDERS OF WADDELL'S WORLD

Farmer Duck • Illustrated by Helen Oxenbury

The Pig In The Pond • Illustrated by Jill Barton
(Note: In this book, a character removes all his clothing. Please preview for appropriateness for your class.)

The Park In The Dark • Illustrated by Barbara Firth
(This book is out of print. Check your library.)

Small Bear Lost • Illustrated by Virginia Austin

Bookmarks
Use with "Welcome To Waddell's World" on page 118.

Share A Book, Share An Experience

Share a Martin Waddell book with your child and you'll share a meaningful childhood experience filled with fun, adventure, and emotion.

These works by Waddell are published by Candlewick Press.

You And Me, Little Bear
Illustrated by Barbara Firth

Sam Vole And His Brothers
Illustrated by Barbara Firth

When The Teddy Bears Came
Illustrated by Penny Dale

The Big Big Sea
Illustrated by Jennifer Eachus

John Joe And The Big Hen
Illustrated by Paul Howard

Once There Were Giants
Illustrated by Penny Dale
(Note: You might choose to substitute a different beverage name for the word *beer* in this story.)

Share A Book, Share An Experience

Share a Martin Waddell book with your child and you'll share a meaningful childhood experience filled with fun, adventure, and emotion.

These works by Waddell are published by Candlewick Press.

You And Me, Little Bear
Illustrated by Barbara Firth

Sam Vole And His Brothers
Illustrated by Barbara Firth

When The Teddy Bears Came
Illustrated by Penny Dale

The Big Big Sea
Illustrated by Jennifer Eachus

John Joe And The Big Hen
Illustrated by Paul Howard

Once There Were Giants
Illustrated by Penny Dale
(Note: You might choose to substitute a different beverage name for the word *beer* in this story.)

©The Education Center, Inc. • *The Best Of The MAILBOX® Authors* • *Pre/K* • TEC1468

Books By Rosemary Wells

On the topic of writing and illustrating children's books, Rosemary Wells was quoted in Something About The Author *as saying, "There are hard parts but no bad or boring parts, and that is more than can be said for any other line of work I know." It's also safe to say that there are no bad or boring parts in the stories that she creates for children. In fact, she helps the readers of her books focus on the humor, the irony, and the tenderness of moments in the life of a child. All of Rosemary Wells's books have unique appeal to young readers, and many have received well-deserved acclaim.*

Pick and choose from among these easy-to-implement ideas to enrich your youngsters' introduction to books by Rosemary Wells.

Timothy Goes To School

Published by Dial Books For Young Readers

Fits Me To A *T*

Poor Timothy! It's the first week of school, and he can't quite live up to the standards of Claude—the class know-it-all. But it doesn't take him long to discover that he can find comfort in a less superficial friendship. Claude has definite feelings about appropriate attire for specific school days. Have each student draw and color a large paper T-shirt cutout to resemble his own favorite T-shirt. Then hang the shirts on a clothesline of yarn using colorful clothespins.

This same activity may be used as a follow-up to *Max's Dragon Shirt.*

Rita Beiswenger—Preschool
Crescent Avenue Weekday School
Fort Wayne, IN

Shy Charles

Published by Dial Books For Young Readers

Shy, But Responsible

Many children experience discomfort associated with being shy, which is part of the reason why your students will love *Shy Charles.* Read the book aloud; then discuss with your youngsters what it means and how it feels to be shy. Find out why they think people sometimes feel shy and how parents generally react to shyness. Then talk about times when it is important not to be shy—like when Charles was courageous enough to get help for his sitter. Assist each child in making a mouse-ears headband. Then give each student an opportunity to participate in a reenactment of the story. Even your shy students will be eager to participate.

Kathy Barton, Altus Public Schools, Altus, OK

Benjamin And Tulip

Published by Dial Books For Young Readers

What Did They Say?

Youngsters may be interested to know that the expressions of the characters in *Benjamin And Tulip* were inspired by Rosemary Wells's West Highland white terrier. After reading this story aloud, have students speculate about the conversation that Benjamin and Tulip are having on the last two pages of the story. Photocopy the pages (and enlarge them if possible); then write in several different conversations as your students dictate. Have youngsters vote to determine their favorite version.

adapted from an idea by Carol Davis—Gr. K
Garrison Elementary School
Savannah, GA

Noisy Nora

Published by Dial Books For Young Readers

Noisy And Quiet

This heartwarming tale of a young mouse who feels neglected is certain to be a favorite of your youngsters. After reading *Noisy Nora* aloud, have students brainstorm activities that are quiet (coloring, reading silently) and activities that are noisy (playing rhythm instruments, dumping out blocks). Make a list of the activities as students mention them. From the list, have each student select a quiet activity in which to participate. Tape-record students as they do each of several quiet activities. Then have each student select a noisy activity. Once again tape youngsters as they participate in each of several noisy activities. Afterwards, replay the tape, giving students opportunities to comment on the noise level of each activity.

Kathy Barton, Altus Public Schools
Altus, OK

All In The Family

In *Noisy Nora,* the main character is trying to get attention from the members of her family. Each of her family members is as different as the persons in your students' families. Have each student make a book entitled "All About My Family." In her book, have each student draw a picture of her family members and herself, featuring one person per page. Near the bottom of each page, have the student write (or dictate for you to write) about each person's favorite activities, usual behaviors, and other characteristics of interest to the child. Provide different media (paints, markers, colored pencils, chalk) for students to use to color their illustrations. Have each student staple her pages between covers that she has designed and colored herself.

Debra Lynn Dechaine, Terryville, CT

The Order Of Things

This booklet is a great medium for having students retell parts of *Noisy Nora* in sequential pictures. Begin by reading aloud *Noisy Nora.* Then, for each youngster, provide a stapled and titled booklet of four pages trimmed and labeled as shown. After writing his name on the cover, have each student draw pictures to represent three sequential events from the story on the respective pages. When students take these booklets home, they'll be anxious to retell the story and to share their illustrations as they do.

Carol Davis—Gr. K, Garrison Elementary School
Savannah, GA

Favorites In A Big-Book Format

Noisy Nora is such a small book that it will add to youngsters' enjoyment to include its finest moments in a really big mouse-shaped big book. Have students decorate mouse-shaped front and back tagboard covers to resemble a mouse. Then, on a mouse-shaped book page, ask each student to illustrate his favorite part of the story, to write about it using inventive spelling, and to sign his page. Stack and number the pages. Using another mouse-shaped page, create a table of contents. Assemble the table of contents and the student pages between the covers. No doubt this book will be a big hit with youngsters, helping them recall *Noisy Nora* as they take pride in their contributions.

Carol Davis—Gr. K

Stanley And Rhoda

Published by Dial Books For Young Readers

A Clean Room

For many youngsters, cleaning their rooms may be one of their most challenging tasks. Room cleaning is the topic of the first of three delightful tales contained in *Stanley And Rhoda.* After reading "Bunny Berries" to your students, have students compare the tasks that Stanley completed with those that Rhoda completed. Ask students to explain why Stanley would have knocked over the bead jar after he had worked so hard to get the room clean. What was he upset about? Have each student draw his room at its messiest; then have him illustrate it again when it has just been cleaned. Ask each student to dictate how he feels in each setting.

A Lion For Lewis

Published by Dial Books For Young Readers
(This book is out of print. Check your library.)

Starring Roles

In *A Lion For Lewis,* Lewis always ends up with the most unattractive roles when he plays with George and Sophie. Each of your youngsters has probably found himself in a similar spot at least once. Ask each youngster who or what his favorite character would be, if he could play the part of anything or anyone that he chose. Then give each youngster a large star cutout on which to draw and color his favorite starring role. Attach a photocopy of a picture of each student to a bulletin board titled "Our Favorite Roles." Atop each child's picture staple his drawing so that the bottom of the drawing can be lifted to reveal his identity. Give children opportunities to look at each drawing and try to guess which of their classmates covets that role.

Hazel's Amazing Mother

Published by Dial Books For Young Readers

Bullies Beware

Although Hazel's doll is handmade, she loves it very much. And when a trio of bullies damages the doll beyond recognition, Hazel's mother comes to the rescue, making them rectify their wrongs. After reading *Hazel's Amazing Mother,* ask your youngsters if they've ever been the victim of bullies, as Hazel was. Ask youngsters to brainstorm how the bullies probably felt as they harassed Hazel. Find out how the bullies' feelings probably changed when they were bullied around by Hazel's mother. Have students role-play the end of the story so that Doris and the boys show better manners and courtesy.

Celebrating Wells's Books

Complete your study of Rosemary Wells's books with your pick of this culminating activity related to her books. Prepare an empty graph with the names of Wells's characters that your students have read about. Have each student indicate which character he liked the best. Graph the responses. Ask students to explain what traits made their favorite characters most appealing.

Sharon Roop—Gr. K
Slate Hill Elementary
Worthington, OH

Kristen Roop—Chapter I
Colonial Hills
Worthington, OH

Additional Books By Rosemary Wells

Published by Dial Books
For Young Readers

Bunny Money
Don't Spill It Again, James
Hooray For Max
Max's Bath
Max's Birthday
Max's Breakfast
Max's Chocolate Chicken
Max's Dragon Shirt
Max's First Word
Max's Ride
Max's Toys: A Counting Book
Waiting For The Evening Star

From **TIMOTHY GOES TO SCHOOL** by Rosemary Wells, copyright ©1981 by Rosemary Wells. Reprinted by permission of Penguin Putnam Books for Young Readers.

AWESOME Audrey Wood

Audrey Wood is a fourth-generation artist whose earliest memories are of the Ringling Brothers Circus. As an infant, she watched her father, an art student, repaint giant big top and sideshow murals. Her mother told her stories about the people that the murals featured. Later her family joined a band of Gypsies on their way to San Miguel, Mexico, where her father had won an art scholarship.

Because she was so creative and different, Audrey was socially out of step with her peers. In her teens, Audrey found more outlets for her creativity, and later she pursued her art career independently. In 1968, she met Don Wood, who became her husband and collaborator. Working together, they created numerous fine books—including *King Bidgood's In The Bathtub, The Napping House,* and *Piggies.*

Illustration excerpts from SILLY SALLY, copyright © 1992 Audrey Wood, reproduced by permission of Harcourt Brace & Company.

King Bidgood's In The Bathtub
Illustrated by Don Wood
Published by Harcourt Brace Jovanovich

It's rub-a-dub trouble when his royal highness refuses to get out of the tub. Read this Caldecott Honor Book aloud to students, stopping with the story's final question, "Who knows what to do?" Challenge each of your youngsters to think of a suggestion for getting the king out of the tub. Then have each student illustrate his proposal. Encourage each of your youngsters to share his picture with the class and explain his proposal. Reread *King Bidgood's In The Bathtub* in its entirety, and get your youngsters' reactions to the ending.

Carol B. Davis—Gr. K
Garrison Elementary School, Savannah, GA

Like King Bidgood, each of your youngsters may have experienced the desire to retreat beneath billowy bubbles—and stay there. To make a sudsy soak picture, begin by coloring a six-inch paper plate to make a self-portrait. Trace a 16-inch footed tub cutout onto construction paper and cut on the resulting outline. Glue the tub cutout to a large sheet of art paper. Then glue on the paper-plate portrait. Use sponge-tip dot applicators, such as bingo markers, to make circular imprints on and above the tub cutout to resemble bubbles. If desired, program the tub with the repetitive lines from the story in which King Bidgood's name has been replaced by the name of the student whose portrait is featured.

Barb Nephew—Gr. K
Beekmantown Central School
Plattsburgh, NY

Help! Help! Rebecca's in the bathtub, and she won't get out. Who knows what to do?

Weird Parents
Published by Dial Books For Young Readers

At one time or another, most kids get the impression that their parents are weird. After having your students offer several different definitions for *weird,* read aloud *Weird Parents.* Then ask youngsters if they think the boy in the story really had weird parents. Find out if youngsters think the boy was lucky or unlucky to have these parents. Ask each of your youngsters to think of one person he knows (other than a classmate) whom he considers to be weird. On a piece of tagboard, have him draw a picture that shows what makes the person weird. Then ask him to think of something about that person that is (or may be) special or wonderful and draw a picture to depict this on the back of the first illustration. Provide confetti, snips of tissue paper, and ribbon, and have each student "frame" each of the illustrations using these materials. To create a colorful suspended display, hang each student's artwork from the ceiling along with a banner that says, "Weird, but wonderful!"

Uncle Frank dances really weird.

Uncle Frank likes to pull my wagon.

Piggies
Cowritten with Don Wood
Illustrated by Don Wood
Published by Harcourt Brace Jovanovich

Read aloud *Piggies* to bring the little piggies fingers-and-toes analogy to life as it has never been done before. Give your youngsters lots of time to analyze the pictures and talk about what the pigs are doing. Then have each youngster press one or both hands into tempera paint and onto art paper. When the paint has dried, have each child decide whether his piggies will be hot, cold, clean, or dirty. Then have him use markers to draw and color some active little piggies on his handprints.

The Napping House
Illustrated by Don Wood
Published by Harcourt Brace Jovanovich

The Napping House will be such a big hit with your little ones, that you'll want to encourage them to share the tale with others. To make retelling the story a lot of fun, help each of your students make these foldout booklets featuring the story line of *The Napping House.* To make a booklet, accordion-fold a 48" x 6" strip of paper so that it is folded into six equal segments. Glue a personalized copy of the roof cutout (page 126) to the first segment. Unfold the paper strip. On each of six 5-inch squares of paper, draw and color a different character from *The Napping House.* Beginning with the bottom segment of the folded strip, glue the characters—one per segment—in the order that they appear in the story. Program each segment of the strip to correspond with the action and characters in the story. When each child has made this napping house booklet, he can retell the story again and again using it as a visual aid.

Renee Amaral—Gr. K
Juan de Anza Elementary, Hawthorne, CA

After reading aloud *The Napping House,* use a similar cumulative story line to help your students develop an original tale. Ask the youngsters what was taking place in the napping house. Then ask them to think of other typical things that might go on in the same house. Choose one of the activities that the youngsters mention to be the focus of a student-made book patterned after *The Napping House.* Youngsters may decide that their book will be about eating, working, or playing, for example. Once the focus is determined, have students brainstorm words that are synonymous with it. List the words on the board. Then—after assigning individuals or small groups of students specific assignments—have each student contribute to a student-made booklet that's a spin-off of *The Napping House.*

This is a house, a munching house,

Where everyone is eating.

Jennifer Barton—Gr. K, Waterbury, CT

More Books By Audrey Wood

Silly Sally (Published by Harcourt Brace Jovanovich)
Heckedy Peg (Published by Harcourt Brace Jovanovich)
Oh My Baby Bear! (Published by Harcourt Brace Jovanovich)
Presto Change-O (Published by Child's Play)
Rude Giants (Published by Harcourt Brace & Company)
Little Mouse, The Red Ripe Strawberry & The Big Hungry Bear—Cowritten with Don Wood (Published by Child's Play)

Little Penguin's Tale
Published by Harcourt Brace Jovanovich

Read aloud *Little Penguin's Tale.* Point out that sometimes when we make mistakes, there is physical evidence that we shouldn't have done what we did. The penguin's missing tail feathers were a good example of this. Most youngsters have probably made a careless mistake that yielded physical results. Give each youngster a tan cutout that resembles a self-adhesive bandage. In the center section, have him draw a picture that illustrates a mistake he made. As the student dictates, write what he learned from the illustrated mistake. Write this dictation on the sides of the imitation bandage.

I should not have been running. I tripped and fell.

My knee is sore. Next time I'll walk.

The Tickleoctopus
Illustrated by Don Wood
Published by Harcourt Brace & Company

Deep in his cavern home, a young caveboy made a delightful discovery. Lurking in the depths of a pond at the back of the cave was a creature that started a chain reaction that changed the course of human history forever. After reading the story, ask the youngsters to pretend that the Tickleoctopus is still alive. Show students a feather boa (or a suitable substitute such as a pink strip of fabric) that has been securely attached to the inside of a classroom closet door so that it protrudes into the classroom. Invite volunteers to take a turn holding the imitation Tickleoctopus tentacle and tell a story about something that made someone smile, laugh, or play. When the storytelling is done, invite youngsters to bring in pictures, books, or other things that make people smile, laugh, or have fun. Display each of these things on or near the door where the Tickleoctopus tentacle is located.

Roof Pattern

Use with *The Napping House* on page 125.

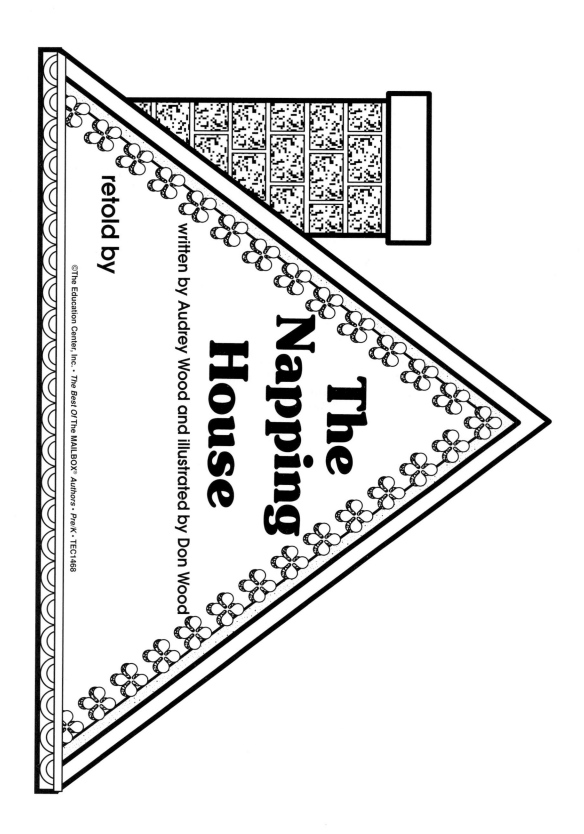

The Napping House

written by Audrey Wood and illustrated by Don Wood

retold by

©The Education Center, Inc. • *The Best Of The MAILBOX® Authors* • Pre/K • TEC1468

The Wondrous Works Of
Jane Yolen

Invite your youngsters to share the fantastical world of Jane Yolen. Through stories ranging from simple concept books to fanciful legends and folktales, this talented poet and storyteller captivates and entertains readers of all ages. Jane Yolen possesses the ability to enchant an audience with her keen sense of wonder, beauty, and humor. So open a book penned by Yolen and be prepared—a fantastic flight into the world of magic and wonder awaits!

Photo by Jason Stemple, 1993

A Sip Of Aesop
Illustrated by Karen Barbour
Published by The Blue Sky Press

Help your youngsters to a delightful serving of Aesop's tales when you share selections from this collection of humorous and witty verse. To extend the tale of "The Lion And The Mouse," have the children discuss the subject of friendship. Assure students that, although they may be small, each of them can offer friendship to anyone. Encourage them to consider the many ways they can be friends to others, large and small alike. Then give each child a sheet of paper programmed with "To other folks, I may seem small, but I can be a friend to all!" Have him illustrate a way in which he can show friendship. After describing his illustration to the class, help each student mount his picture on a bulletin-board display with the title "A Friend To All."

To other folks, I may be small, but I can be a friend to all!

Piggins
Illustrated by Jane Dyer
Published by Harcourt Brace Jovanovich, Publishers

Students will be inspired to use their own problem-solving skills after hearing this story about how Piggins, a wise and proper butler, solves the mystery of the missing *lavaliere* (necklace). To prepare a lavaliere for this activity, hot-glue a plastic gemstone to a length of ribbon. During group time, explain to students that they will each have an opportunity to solve the mystery of the missing lavaliere. Invite a student volunteer to play the role of Piggins. Have that child leave the room. While he is away, invite another child to take the lavaliere and hide it in his pocket, under his shirt, or elsewhere on his person. Then have the child posing as Piggins return. Explain that there is a thief among the group, and it is up to Piggins to identify him! Provide "Piggins" with clues, one at a time, to help him identify the thief. The clues may include information such as the thief's gender, hair color, or a description of his clothing. When the thief is identified, invite him to assume the role of Piggins. Continue in this manner until every child has had an opportunity to solve the mystery of the missing lavaliere.

Dawn Spurck, Educational Service Unit #3, Omaha, NE

For additional detective fun, challenge students to embark on a search for clues to unravel an even greater mystery—the disappearance of a classroom treasure! If desired, prepare a detective badge for each student to wear during this activity. In advance, arrange for your school's principal or another staff member to pose as the thief. Set a tentative time for this person to be "caught" in possession of the missing item, which may be a stapler, tape recorder, or some other familiar classroom item. Then hide clues in various locations around your class and school. Arrange the sequence and hiding places of the clues so that each clue leads the children to the next clue. For example, the first clue may be a large tennis shoe found where the missing item would typically be located. Prompt youngsters to decide on a location in the school where a large tennis shoe may be found, such as in the gym. When they look in the gym, help them discover the next clue, such as a milk carton. Then have the class go to the location where they would most likely find a milk carton—to discover still another clue. After discovering a series of clues in this manner, have the students follow the last clue to the location of the thief. When the group arrives at that location, have the guilty party sporting some form of evidence to prove him guilty, such as wearing the matching tennis shoe. On discovering this final piece of evidence, encourage students to request that the thief return the missing treasure. Case solved!

Detective Nancy

Nancy Kriener, Fillmore Central Elementary School, Preston, MN

Owl Moon
Illustrated by John Schoenherr
Published by Philomel Books

What better time to go owling than on a cold, quiet, winter night lit up by the light of the moon? This is just what a young girl and her father do in this engaging tale about a fascinating nocturnal pastime. After reading this story aloud, encourage youngsters to practice their auditory memory skills with this listening game. Have the students form a circle. Explain that one child will produce an owl call, then will shine a flashlight at the chest of another child. That child will repeat the call made by the first child. Then the child who reproduced the call will take the flashlight, produce a different owl call, and then shine the light at another student. As the children play, encourage them to produce different rhythmic patterns using the short and long "whoo" sounds of an owl. Continue play until every child has had the opportunity to produce and repeat an owl-call pattern. Youngsters will have a hooting good time with this one!

Old Dame Counterpane
Illustrated by Ruth Tietjen Councell
Published by Philomel Books

From sunrise to sunset, Old Dame Counterpane rocks and sews, sews and rocks, creating an evergrowing earth full of color and life from a ten-square quilt. But what will Dame Counterpane do when the last stitch is applied and her quilt is spread over the night? Read this colorful verse aloud to students; then invite them to help create a class quilt. To prepare, write each number from one to ten on a separate square sheet of poster board. Give each student a 9" x 9" square of white construction paper. Assign him a number from one to ten. Then have him draw a picture to depict one of the creations mentioned in the story for his assigned number. When the pictures are completed, mount each to the poster-board square corresponding to the appropriate number. Hole-punch several holes along the side edges of each square; then sequence them in a row. In quilt-fashion, attach the poster squares to one another by lacing ribbon through the holes. Display the class quilt with the title "Sew Up The Day With Old Dame Counterpane."

Mouse's Birthday
Illustrated by Bruce Degen
Published by G. P. Putnam's Sons

Mouse lives in a very small house—so small, in fact, that all his friends barely fit in it for his birthday celebration! But fit they do! And the celebration is held, with the traditional cake and candle-lighting. Oh, what a surprise for the entire party when Mouse blows out the candle! And what fun your youngsters will have as they role-play this delightful story! After reading the story aloud, spread out a parachute (or a large flat sheet) to represent Mouse's house. Have your students kneel around the edges of the parachute. Assign the role of each character from the story to a child. Have the child playing the role of Mouse sit under the parachute. Then ask each child who is assigned a character role to crawl under the parachute according to the sequence in the story. When all the children portraying the characters are under the parachute, have them call out "Happy Birthday, Mouse," then pretend to blow out a candle. As the children under the parachute blow, encourage the students kneeling around the outer edges of the parachute to simultaneously lift and release the parachute into the air. Now Mouse's house is wide—wide enough for all of his friends, and even more, to fit inside! Replace the parachute and repeat the activity so that each student has an opportunity to role-play a character.

Dawn Spurck
Educational Service Unit #3
Omaha, NE

More Jane Yolen Books

Eeny, Meeny, Miney Mole
Illustrated by Kathryn Brown
Published by
Harcourt Brace Jovanovich

Baby Bear's Bedtime Book
Illustrated by Jane Dyer
Published by
Harcourt Brace Jovanovich

An Invitation To The Butterfly Ball
Illustrated by Jane Breskin Zalben
Published by Boyd's Mills Press